Castoriadis, Foucault, and Autonomy

"Cornelius Castoriadis was one of the most original and imaginative social thinkers of the twentieth century. Focusing on the themes of subject, society, and social change, Tovar-Restrepo has written a lucid and lively exposition and defense of his engaged thinking. Comparing him with Foucault she argues that Castoriadis helps to solve fundamental problems that Foucault left unresolved. This is an excellent contribution in restoring the importance of the thinker of radical imagination and radical democracy!"
Richard J. Bernstein, Vera List Professor of Philosophy, New School For Social Research, New York, USA

"In a discussion of the highest intellectual quality, Tovar-Restrepo explicates Castoriadis' principal ideas, placing the development of his thought in its historical and political context, and engaging critically with the ongoing debates surrounding his work. In comparing Castoriadis' thought with that of the more widely-known Foucault, she uncovers the strengths and weaknesses of each, and presents a persuasive case for the under-recognized value of Castoriadis' thought for understanding the human subject and society, and as an intellectual foundation for the political project of autonomy. This book is an important addition to the growing body of scholarship on Castoriadis' thought and a valuable contribution to the critical appraisal of Foucault."
Jeff Klooger, Swinburne University of Technology, Australia, author of *Castoriadis: Psyche, Society, Autonomy*

"In a close reading of these works, Tovar-Restrepo gives a rigorous and passionate account of a fundamental debate in French contemporary philosophy."
Fabio Ciaramelli, Professor of Legal Philosophy, University of Catania, Italy

"Tovar-Restrepo's reading of Castoriadis, a lesser-known contemporary of Foucault, is clear, concise, and critically thought-provoking."
Vincent Crapanzano, Distinguished Professor of Comparative Literature and Anthropology at the Graduate Center of the City University of New York, USA

Continuum Studies in Continental Philosophy

Series Editor: James Fieser, University of Tennessee at Martin, USA

Continuum Studies in Continental Philosophy is a major monograph series from Continuum. The series features first-class scholarly research monographs across the field of Continental philosophy. Each work makes a major contribution to the field of philosophical research.

Adorno's Concept of Life, Alastair Morgan
Badiou, Marion and St Paul, Adam Miller
Being and Number in Heidegger's Thought, Michael Roubach
Deleuze and Guattari, Fadi Abou-Rihan
Deleuze and the Genesis of Representation, Joe Hughes
Deleuze and the Unconscious, Christian Kerslake
Deleuze, Guattari and the Production of the New, edited by Simon O'Sullivan and Stephen Zepke
Derrida, Simon Morgan Wortham
Derrida and Disinterest, Sean Gaston
Derrida: Profanations, Patrick O'Connor
The Domestication of Derrida, Lorenzo Fabbri
Encountering Derrida, edited by Simon Morgan Wortham and Allison Weiner
Foucault's Heidegger, Timothy Rayner
Gadamer and the Question of the Divine, Walter Lammi
Heidegger and a Metaphysics of Feeling, Sharin N. Elkholy
Heidegger and Aristotle, Michael Bowler
Heidegger and Logic, Greg Shirley
Heidegger and Nietzsche, Louis P. Blond
Heidegger and Philosophical Atheology, Peter S. Dillard
Heidegger Beyond Deconstruction, Michael Lewis
Heidegger, Politics and Climate Change, Ruth Irwin
Heidegger's Early Philosophy, James Luchte
Idealism and Existentialism, Jon Stewart
Kant, Deleuze and Architectonics, Edward Willatt
Levinas and Camus, Tal Sessler
Merleau-Ponty's Phenomenology, Kirk M. Besmer
Nietzsche's Ethical Theory, Craig Dove
Nietzsche, Nihilism and the Philosophy of the Future, edited by Jeffrey Metzger
Nietzsche's Thus Spoke Zarathustra, edited by James Luchte
The Philosophy of Exaggeration, Alexander Garcia Düttmann
Sartre's Phenomenology, David Reisman
Time and Becoming in Nietzsche's Thought, Robin Small
Who's Afraid of Deleuze and Guattari? Gregg Lambert
Žižek and Heidegger, Thomas Brockelman
Žižek's Dialectics, Fabio Vighi

Castoriadis, Foucault, and Autonomy
New Approaches to Subjectivity, Society, and Social Change

Marcela Tovar-Restrepo

Continuum Studies in Continental Philosophy

Continuum International Publishing Group
The Tower Building   80 Maiden Lane
11 York Road   Suite 704
London SE1 7NX   New York NY 10038

www.continuumbooks.com

© Marcela Tovar-Restrepo 2012

All rights reserved. No part of this publication may be reproduced
or transmitted in any form or by any means, electronic or mechanical,
including photocopying, recording, or any information storage or
retrieval system, without prior permission in writing from the publishers.

The author has asserted his/her right under the Copyright, Designs and Patents
Act, 1988, to be identified as Author of this work.

British Library Cataloguing-in-Publication Data
A catalogue record for this book is available from the British Library.

ISBN: HB: 978-1-4411-3404-2

Library of Congress Cataloguing-in-Publication Data
Tovar-Restrepo, Marcela.
Castoriadis, Foucault, and autonomy: new approaches to subjectivity, society, and
social change/Marcela Tovar-Restrepo.
    p. cm. – (Continuum studies in Continental philosophy)
Includes bibliographical references (p.) and index.
ISBN 978-1-4411-3404-2 (hardcover)
1. Castoriadis, Cornelius, 1922–1997. 2. Foucault, Michel, 1926–1984. I. Title.
B2430.C3584T68 2011
194–dc23   2011037081

Typeset by Deanta Global Publishing Services, Chennai, India
Printed and bound in Great Britain

For Pablo Tovar and María del Pilar Restrepo

Contents

Acknowledgments	viii
Introduction	1
Chapter 1: The Socialisme ou Barbarie Period (1949–65)	9
Chapter 2: Cornelius Castoriadis' Ontology of Creation	33
Chapter 3: Agency and Autonomy in Castoriadis	65
Chapter 4: Michel Foucault: The Game of Power and Resistance	91
Chapter 5: Society Over the Subject	115
Chapter 6: Castoriadis versus Foucault: Concluding Remarks	133
Notes	141
Bibliography	151
Index	161

Acknowledgments

I would like to express my gratitude to Richard Bernstein, Joel Whitebook, Vincent Crapanzano, Fabio Giraldo, and Andreas Kalyvas, for their steady support and intellectual interlocution.

I would also like to thank Zoé Castoriadis, Myrto Gondicas, Enrique Escobar, and David Curtis for lending me access to privileged information about Cornelius Castoriadis' life and personal archives in Paris. Laurie Naranch, Rafael Miranda, José Malaver, Jeff Klooger, and Suzi Adams also contributed toward making this project possible.

I am indebted to Stephanie Damoff who did previous copyediting of this manuscript and successfully overcame the challenging task of working with Cornelius Castoriadis' neologisms.

Finally, for generous company, joy, and good sense of humor, I would like to thank my family and friends whose presence is throughout this work. I am especially grateful to Pablo Tovar, María del Pilar Restrepo, Ana María Tovar, Sofía Samper, Emilio Samper, Jordi Castello, Carlos Moreno-Leguizamón, and Jorge G. Castañeda.

Introduction

Ici encore Kant avait vu la chose, bien qu'il l'ait travestie, lorsqu'il disait que l'œuvre d'art est « présentation dans l'intuition des Idées de la Raison ». Car ce que l'art présente, ce ne sont pas les Idées de la Raison, mais le Chaos, l'Abîme, le Sans Fond, à quoi il donne forme. Et par cette présentation, il est fenêtre sur le Chaos, il abolit l'assurance tranquillement stupide de notre vie quotidienne, il nous rappelle que nous vivons toujours au bord de l'Abîme - ce qui est le principal savoir d'un être autonome.

Cornelius Castoriadis, 'La Culture dans une Société Démocratique'

> What art presents are not the Ideas of Reason [as Kant believed] but the Chaos, the Abyss, the Groundlessness to which it gives form. And through this presentation, it is a window on the Chaos; it abolishes our tranquil and stupid assurance about our daily life; it reminds us that we forever live at the edge of the Abyss—which is the main thing an autonomous being knows.

Cornelius Castoriadis, 'Culture in a Democratic Society'

Hobbes avait raison, mais pas pour ses raisons à lui. La peur de la mort est la pierre angulaire des institutions. Non pas la peur d'être tué par le voisin – mais la peur, tout à fait justifiée, que tout, même le sens, se dissoudra.

Cornelius Castoriadis, 'Psychanalyse et Politique'

> Hobbes was right though for the wrong reason. Fear of death is indeed the main state of institution. Not fear of being killed by the next man but the justified fear that everything, even meaning will dissolve.

Cornelius Castoriadis, 'Psychoanalysis and Politics'

Michel Foucault and Cornelius Castoriadis' social theories arose as products of postwar French modernization, a fruitful moment for prolific and multifarious intellectual productions. The work of both authors was informed by the rapidly changing conditions experienced in France during the 1950s–70s. Modernist views, Fordism, and industrialization transformed France into an urban country that no longer ruled colonies and that was acquiring new forms of centralized development and regulated labor relations. After 1945, the French state set about designing and implementing policies and institutional arrangements to ensure economic growth and financial stability. New patterns of mass production and consumption significantly changed the socioeconomic French scenario which became a central problem to be analyzed in the light of social and revolutionary theory, for French thinkers such as Cornelius Castoriadis and his group Socialisme ou Barbarie (SouB).[1]

A flourishing intellectual atmosphere accompanied these changes. During this period, France hosted rich debates animated by the resurgence of Hegelianism after World War ll. For many intellectuals and leftists, Hegel's *Phenomenology of Spirit* was an important source for a needed renewal in the social and political arenas, including Marxist historical materialism (Poster, 1975, pp. 5, 51–61; Lichtheim, 1966, p. 81).

Reintroduced in France by Alexandre Kojève and Jean Hyppolite at l'École des hautes études en sciences sociales, authors like Maurice Merleau-Ponty, Jacques Lacan, Michel Foucault, Gilles Deleuze, Louis Althusser, and Jacques Derrida benefited from this discussion. Studying Hegel allowed a critical reflection on the crucial contents present at the core of modernist thought, such as the Cartesian legacy and some romantic notions.[2] This debate, along with the need to respond to the exhaustion of Marxism, informed emerging trends that shaped the theoretical and political French milieu of the 1960s and 1970s when Foucault and Castoriadis began to produce their bodies of work. Philosophical developments such as Sartre's existentialism, Merleau-Ponty's phenomenology, Lacan's Freudian reinterpretation, and even the preceding Levi-Straussian structuralism—just to name a few—were some of the of theories produced contemporaneously with Foucault's and Castoriadis' writings.

Even though Foucault and Castoriadis' formative and productive years shared similar contextual conditions, their intellectual and private trajectories greatly differed. Coming from different environments and personal backgrounds, their work followed distinct paths and became consolidated through different institutional dynamics, political organizations, and academic circuits.[3] The way they related to their immediate intellectual context and to the debates taking place in France and abroad proved to be crucial for shaping their differences and similarities, and to the way they were received and positioned among the public.

From early on, different personal and political experiences in their youth contributed toward shaping their philosophical concerns and critical perspectives. While as an adolescent Castoriadis joined leftist political organizations and initiated a prolonged militancy that encouraged his interest in social theory and, more specifically in Marxism, Foucault turned to more personal concerns that took him into the study of psychology and the exploration of institutional forms that dealt with mental disorders. Their initial intellectual influences and training reflected their dissimilar interests, upon which they also set research agendas that they developed through different projects. Foucault remained working in academic and scholarly environments while Castoriadis turned to political organizations that sought to critically reflect on revolutionary theory and their consequent political militancy.

Castoriadis was born in Constantinople in 1922 and lived in Athens from the time he was three months old. In what was then a small city, Castoriadis spent his childhood in the company of his father, who he described as a Voltairean, anticlerical, antimonarchist democrat who professed great admiration for the French, and his mother, a pianist who taught him musical skills. From his youth, he was familiar with French culture. His father taught him French by making him declaim Francophone poetry and recite Plato's *Apology* while his father shaved in the morning.

Castoriadis was greatly influenced by his family. Early in his life he developed a deep intellectual curiosity. He recalled buying, at age 13, a secondhand book on the history of philosophy, while he also developed great passion for Marxist theory. As an adolescent his political interests led him to secretly buy the communist newspaper and in 1937, during his last year at school, to join a small revolutionary cell of the Communist Youth of Greece. Together with other three comrades, he fought Ioannis Metaxas' dictatorship (1936–41) until his partners were arrested. In that same year Castoriadis entered the law school at the Athens University, where he pursued a career in economics and political science.

In 1941, during the German occupation, he joined the Greek Communist Party where he founded a journal named *Nea Epochi*, aimed at reforming the party from within. Nevertheless, as time passed it became clear to him that the Greek Communist Party was not an independent body but was in line with the Third International, which he opposed. As a result, in 1942 Castoriadis joined the leftist faction of the Greek Trotskyist party led by

Spiros Stinas. His militancy continued until the end of 1945 when he left for France in the famous ship called *Mataroa*, along with other intellectuals like Kostas Axelos.

Some months after his arrival in France, he joined the Trotskyites and organized the Second World Congress of the Fourth International, held in 1948. However, by that time Castoriadis met Claude Lefort, with whom he started questioning Trotsky's conceptions and later founded the group Socialisme ou Barbarie (1949–65).

In 1948, Castoriadis started working at the The Organisation for Economic Co-operation and Development (OECD), where he stayed until 1970. In 1973, he became a practicing psychoanalyst and published his main work, *L'Institution Imaginaire de la Société*, in 1975.

Castoriadis never pursued a traditional academic career despite his active and productive intellectual activity. He was part of the French journals *Textures* (1972–5) and *Libre* (1975–80), and taught economics at Nanterre (1974–6) and philosophy at the L'École des hautes études en sciences sociales (1980–95).

Unlike the then-emerging intellectual figures, Castoriadis did not follow a regular scholarly path. Rather than joining recognized intellectual networks or meeting the requirements of academic life, Castoriadis was a heterodox thinker who concentrated on elaborating on his ideas and less on positioning them. In terms of content, Castoriadis' work was also singular and did not reflect flourishing trends or ideologies. It did not meet expectations common to his immediate political and posthumanist context. On the contrary, he resembled a French encyclopedist whose work requires interdisciplinary knowledge and is not easily categorized. Correctly described as a "*penseur en chaleur*," Castoriadis elaborated and refined his thinking as he progressively wrote and published his *oeuvre*, which precisely because of its heterodoxy and singularity can cause some difficulty to his readers.

Foucault, on the other hand, was a different character. Despite his creativity and originality, his work drew more directly on received theoretical bodies, met widespread academic expectations, and was in dialogue with fashionable poststructuralist authors. Foucault also remained part of diverse and renowned academic circles, and it was not until later that his political activities became an important part of his intellectual life.

Foucault was born in Poitiers (France) in 1926 and was raised in a conservative and well-established middle-class family. In 1943 he completed his secondary education, and entered L'École normale supérieure (ENS) in Paris in 1945. From 1949 to 1951 he pursued his studies in philosophy and entered the psychology program, practicing at the Sainte-Anne psychiatric hospital. He developed an interest in psychopathology and concluded a diploma course in 1952. Between 1954 and 1955 he worked at the University of Lille and at the ENS, followed by work at the University of Uppsala (Sweden) and the Clermont-Ferrand University in 1960–6. He later taught at the University of Tunis (1966–8) and Vincennes University (1968), until he was elected to the Collège de France in 1969.

While teaching, Foucault also did rigorous solitary research at libraries such as the Bibliothèque nationale de France, where he spent long hours. He became a major intellectual figure and a prolific best selling author. His first books, such as *Madness and Civilization* published in 1961, were extensively reviewed and sold out. He also published and contributed to widely recognized journals such as *Tel-Quel, Critique, and Nouvelle Revue Française*.

In his youth, Foucault was not interested in politics. He devoted more time and attention to his personal affairs which his biographers describe as depressive episodes.[4] His personal conditions kept him immersed in private affairs and intellectual activities. In 1950 he joined the French Communist Party but never had an active militancy and left after a few years. Despite his lack of participation in political groups, he was interested in leftist groups and declared his sympathy for political causes. He made declarations against the Algerian and Vietnam wars and against racist practices toward immigrants in France. He also visited Iran to meet Ayatollah Khomeini and initially supported the interim government after the Iranian revolution.

Foucault's more active political life started when his intellectual career was consolidated. It was not until the beginning of the 1970s that the relationship between Foucault's political activity and intellectual work became evident. Through his work with prisoners at the *Group d'information sur les prisons*—the political work he was most devoted to—Foucault expanded his political horizon and increased his activism.

Foucault and Castoriadis never held a public debate about their work. In their writings, mutual quotes are nonexistent. It was quite clear to these living authors that their work and critical perspectives were far apart. Nevertheless, despite their great differences, a parallel relationship and comparison between Foucault and Castoriadis is plausible given that their theoretical productions respond to common philosophical questions. They shared similar challenges and tackled common problems seeking to contest theoretical legacies firmly rooted in their intellectual milieu. Both Castoriadis and Foucault sought to contest modernist and rationalistic perspectives that implied unified and objective realities, absolute values, and transcendental ideas or forms of subjects. They opposed metaphysical philosophical traditions, criticizing any ultimate anthropological foundation, such as reason, or any teleological vision of history or human progress.

Along this line, they sought to explain reality as a social construct through representation, questioning views that presupposed total independence between the cognizant subject and an autonomous reality. They acknowledged the historical, contingent, and relative character of social formations, and negated the ideal of ultimate, unique, and optimal forms of society that reflected the so-called end of history.

Castoriadis and Foucault agreed that the human subject, as well as his or her social reality, was a product of representational activity, where historical and cultural meaning gave life to society while shaping the individual's subjectivity. Even though they supported this premise on different theoretical bases, both authors defended the interpretation of social reality as a representation invested with meaning that gave sense to social practices and institutions. In this respect, Foucault was strongly influenced by the linguistic turn tendency, which drove him to defend the discursive nature of social formations, while Castoriadis formulated an ontology of creation, posing new concepts such as the radical imaginary as the source of imaginary social significations and social institutions.

In this book, I establish a dialogue between Foucault's and Castoriadis' bodies of thought, discussing their potentialities, limitations, and contributions without omitting their differences and convergences. I focus on three main notions that are central for both scholars' theories: the subject, the production of social meaning and representation, and social change. I show the importance of these concepts to each thinker, enabling a better understanding of their theoretical consequences and political implications.

After establishing the main points of comparison, I argue for Castoriadis' philosophical and theoretical position, and present it as an alternative to unresolved poststructuralist problems and to what Castoriadis saw as a deterministic ontology embedded in political relativism. This discussion opens up an invigorating debate about autonomy, subjectivity, power, and agency, pointing out important limitations present in poststructuralism. Castoriadis' theoretical tools allow an original examination under the lens of determinism of those notions as they occur in Foucault's work—an unprecedented analysis of a widely read author about whom much has been written during recent decades. Given the extensive literature available on Foucault, I assume some familiarity on the part of the reader and emphasize Castoriadis' theoretical trajectory, though I do not intend to chronologically trace his conceptual developments. My goal is to enable new understandings of subjectivity, social life, and transformation through an alternative reading of agency and autonomy. Nondeterministic conceptions of the subject, society, and social change should allow us to go beyond mere criticism and attempt to preserve an autonomous position and attitude in the generation of knowledge and social theory.

The discussion is divided into six chapters. Chapter 1 centers on an early period of Castoriadis' life as a young intellectual militant in Paris when, together with other figures like Claude Lefort and Jean-Francois Lyotard, he founded the legendary journal *Socialisme ou Barbarie* (SB) in 1949. The group of the same name, credited as the source of inspiration in May 1968 by Daniel Cohn-Bendit (1968), denounced socialist contradictions and Stalinist authoritarian excesses until 1965 when it dissolved. The group advanced alternative leftist thinking by sharing in and drawing on the experience of French factory workers. In this initial period of his intellectual career, Castoriadis questioned Marxism and set the foundations for the key concepts in his work, particularly the origins of his notions of autonomy, creation, and indetermination. I analyze these concepts in the following chapter, building a bridge between these two moments in Castoriadis' development.

Chapter 2 traces the conceptual path of Castoriadis' ontology of creation, which is known as his main philosophical work and contribution. Here I present its basic concepts, explaining its Freudian and philosophical roots. The ontological status given to imagination in the forms of the radical imagination of the singular psyche and the social instituting/instituted imaginary are also approached and discussed. This chapter goes on to present the leaning-on explanation of the existing-being that substantiates both his concept of creation and its indeterminate character. Here the relation between the psychical and the social poles is explained, including the stratification of the human psyche, as well as critiques made to some of his notions such as the monadic state of the psyche or leaning-on doctrine. Furthermore, as this chapter draws on Castoriadis' main work, *The Imaginary Institution of Society*, the social-historical is addressed as a particular way to re-conceptualize society and history. The social-historical is explained as the creation of the anonymous collective through the existing tension between its instituting and instituted power that distances it from the common perception of society as a sum of individual intersubjective networks.

Chapter 3 focuses on the primary innovative contributions made by Castoriadis with his notions of the subject, agency, the production of social meaning and representation, and social change. It discusses the potentialities, weaknesses, and problems related to these concepts, including critiques made by leading intellectual figures. It also engages with discussions of emerging scholars who pose interesting points of reflection in relation to

Castoriadis' theory. As a corollary of these debates, the notion of autonomy is examined as a social creation that does not constitute an ultimate or transcendental foundation, which poses a different understanding of the normative criteria in the anthropological and political realms, redefining the encounter between norm and fact. Unresolved tensions present in autonomy as both a subjective individual project and as a collective political one, are also approached in the light of contemporary democratic political systems.

Chapter 4 starts by discussing Foucault's work, providing a comprehensive overview of his theory and illustrating his different stands over time with respect to the three main problems with which we are concerned. It takes into account his different foci of analysis: in the 1960s, on systems of knowledge from an archaeological perspective; in the 1970s, on the genealogical approach to modalities of power; and in the 1980s, on technologies of the self, ethics, and freedom. It also reviews further and more developed insights Foucault had in relation to power and how the problem of domination and heteronomy is understood in relation to Castoriadis' understanding. Important notions that underlie both authors' work, such as history and knowledge, are also tackled in a constructive comparison.

Chapter 5 continues discussing Foucault's developments, examining his insights from a Castoridian perspective and revealing important implications and limitations of his poststructuralist assumptions. Foucault's significant findings and weaknesses are analyzed in relation to his arguments on freedom; on the possibility of reconstructing ourselves; on our own subjectivity and subjective constitution; on the differentiation between power and domination; on the productive character of power; and on the continuous questioning he invited. Studied within the Foucauldian theoretical structure, these problems acquire new meanings and repercussions inferred from Castoriadis' position.

Finally, the conclusion sums up the affinities and differences in Foucault and Castoriadis' works as they provide a theoretical basis for a critique of Foucault's legacy. It argues for a Castoridian point of view that tackles the question of determinacy versus indeterminacy in relation to autonomy. It shows how the main contributions made by Castoriadis on the problem of subjectivity and subjective constitution provide fruitful means to consider new conceptualizations of agency, autonomy, and radical democracy. Castoriadis' unique ideas reinstate the project of autonomy—undermined by the social sciences as a residue of the modernist Cartesian and Kantian philosophies of the subject—which then suggests new ways to redirect social theory and social change.

Chapter 1
The Socialisme ou Barbarie Period (1949–65)

The significant relationship between Castoriadis' work during the Socialisme ou Barbarie period and his subsequent development is not self-evident for everyone interested in his *oeuvre*. By including a partial summary of this productive moment in Castoriadis' life, I intend to emphasize a crucial relationship he always established between his political concerns and activities and his intellectual production. In my view, the Socialisme ou Barbarie period allowed Castoriadis to identify the main questions that shaped his later reflections and gave birth to his ontology of creation. This chapter aims to illustrate the way Cornelius Castoriadis' analysis of conjunctural political events led him to develop an original critique of deterministic conceptions of history, theory, and society, as well as revolutionary thinking. Castoriadis' main contributions to the philosophical and political fields, such as the open-ended creativity of history and the ontological weight of imagination—addressed in Chapters 2 and 3—find their origin in the contradictions and aporias Castoriadis recognized as he progressively built an original critique of Marxism and authoritarian socialist regimes. As introduced in this chapter, many of the key notions and philosophical problems that Castoriadis developed after Socialisme ou Barbarie dissolved, were born out of his compromised political militancy. It is the case, for example, that his shop-floor experiences with factory workers not only enriched his analysis of bureaucracy and capitalism, but also set the basis for later concepts such as heteronomy and autonomy.

A synthesis of what I judge as relevant events for Castoriadis' work during the Socialisme ou Barbarie period are presented here. Their periodization is based on a succinct historical account of the group that Castoriadis wrote about (Castoriadis, 1997m, pp. 1–34), though he never published a complete history of the group.

Early Productions of Cornelius Castoriadis: The Socialisme ou Barbarie Period: 1949–65

During the preparatory discussions for the Second Congress of the Fourth International, Castoriadis and Claude Lefort[1] set up in August 1946, there was a tendency to criticize bureaucratic formations in revolutionary organisms within the Communist Party (CP).[2] In 1947, this tendency was found in a dozen comrades who progressively raised questions about relevant issues related to the class struggle, revolutionary theory, and the concept of socialism.

In the summer of 1948, when the group had decided to leave the CP, the break between Tito and the Cominform in Yugoslavia took place. The controversy that Tito's affair brought up demonstrated that the socialist revolution in Eastern European countries was being judged based only on the criteria of nationalization, private property, and planning and the totalitarian power of the Party as the instrument for their realization as central objectives of the revolution.[3] This also contributed to the setting up of the group as an independent organism that published the first issue of *Socialisme ou Barbarie* (*SB*) in 1949.

This group, which also called itself Socialisme ou Barbarie (SouB) became one of the most important French intellectual groups that critically sustained a dialogue with postwar capitalism. Joined by intellectuals like Jean Francois Lyotard, Pierre Souyri, Jean Laplanche, and Daniel Mothé, SouB started to develop their work around topics that influenced the French "New Left."[4]

The small group (20 members) met biweekly at Le Tambour Café in Paris to discuss the production of the journal and its revolutionary project. Their initial work centered around the critique of the bureaucracy in the Soviet Union, the bureaucratic nature of Communist parties, and the analysis of the worldwide capital concentration process that had crystallized into an intransigent conflict between two expansionist super powers, which were characterized by the increasing bureaucratization of their societies as well as their economies. Correlated issues that also inspired them had to do with the relation between critical social analysis and revolutionary politics, the relations between intellectual and manual labor, and between the party and the masses, what it meant to be a militant, and how to define a revolutionary project. SouB addressed these questions within a critical perspective of Marxism[5], framing their discussion on national and international events such as the Cold War, the unrest and popular manifestations against the communist leadership in some Eastern Europe countries, the implications of Gaullism for working-class politics, the Algerian War, and the tiers-mondiste interpretations of the Algerian *Front National de Libération* (FNL), which was fashionable among the students and the antiwar movement.

Until 1958, the group only published their journal, however, at the end of that year they also made a monthly mimeographed supplement: *Pouvoir Ouvrier* (PO). This supplement tried to animate workers' revolutionary reflections and actions, offering assistance to forward the workers' struggles. Around PO, discussion groups that would influence future actions of student–worker rebellions[6] were set up in numerous cities[7] and in the Parisian Latin Quarter (Curtis, 1988, pp. ix–xi; Schnapp and Vidal-Naquet, 1971, p. 65).

The organization and militancy of the group were always questions that referred to the role of revolutionary theory and its formulation. For SouB theory clarified the implications of workers' actions, fitting them into a vision of history-in-the-making leading toward social revolution and the institution of direct democracy. Theory was an instrument for developing self-consciousness and a sense of continuity for the worker. The revolutionary movement therefore had to assimilate the modes of thought implicit in the working-class action and to begin rethinking about the conceptual core of revolutionary theory. In this sense, the workers' organizations, and self-directed worker actions shaped by the everyday experience of worker collectives, were efforts to stake out a new political terrain. SouB had access to the workers and their collective experiences and demands through the compilation, publication, and analysis of worker autobiographies, strike reports, and position papers analyzing political and trade union issues.

Within this approach, SouB sought to contest the way socialism was being experienced in USSR, comparing it to the similar phenomenon produced by the Western capitalist exploiting class. Influenced to some extent by Max Weber, Castoriadis saw that the bureaucracy that had arisen in Russia since 1917 was that of a new ruling class, an exploiting class as oppressive as the Western bourgeoisie. Taking off from its first critiques of Stalinist bureaucracy, SouB radicalized their position by drawing a connection between Stalin's state and Lenin's theory of organization. In both cases the same problem operated: the workers were objectified and seen as passive social elements. Castoriadis saw this problem in both Western capitalism and the Russian state, not simply confined to the means of production, but also in the bureaucratic nature of its social relations.

SouB intended to maintain and rethink the revolutionary project while being critical of the official left, the experiences of Eastern European countries under the Red Army, Tito's Yugoslavia, the Hungarian revolution in 1956 and, as said, the USSR in general. Castoriadis was highly critical of the USSR's authoritative regime and claimed that the Soviet Union was not only a degenerate workers' state, but represented a new form of class oppression. For him the USSR was neither a socialist union nor a republic. In effect, with the belief that a critical examination of the USSR was essential in order to keep revolutionary theory as a coherent orientation for postwar militants, the group sought to distinguish itself from other leftist groups, including Trotskyism, by positioning themselves ideologically close to the working class. The regime in USSR was interpreted as a new type that had nothing to do with socialism and being constituted around a bureaucratic and authoritarian party. The soviet system was the end state toward which Western bureaucratic capitalism was being borne by the logic of concentration. The group related this bureaucracy to the structure of the Leninist party, where there was a division of intellectual and manual work legitimated by the left. In contrast, SouB tried to rethink socialism as a direct democracy. Its contents derived from the group's close analysis of working-class actions in opposition to both capitalist organization and conventional politics.

Most of their analyses were based on the development course of Fordism in France and other international experiences that provided them a broader scope for their theoretical achievements. By analyzing the effects of Fordist industrial organization, SouB sought to uncover what they saw as potential for new patterns of revolutionary action that were posited in the course of everyday experience at the point of production. What made SouB an example of a counter-history of Fordism was the attention they paid to social relations, as well as their treatment of those relations as originating a new revolutionary project where self-conscious historical actors were protagonists. Based on the autobiographical accounts they had gathered of workers' experiences in factories, SouB reformulated the Marxist problem of class formation and its relation to worker experience, rethinking in this way about political possibilities for change (Hastings-King, 1999, pp. 45–9).

Castoriadis saw workers as creative participants in the building of socialism, which he defined as people's conscious organization of their own life in all domains. Hence, SouB turned to the tradition of workers' councils in forming their concept of a revolutionary organization. Castoriadis emphasized the critical concepts of workers' self-management and alienation as means of de-bureaucratizing socialist movements: socialism should not merely try to transform relations at the workplace but should transform and democratize all areas of social life. SouB followed a trajectory that went from a critique of Stalinism and Leninism to a critique of contemporary capitalism, emphasizing the need for overturning all alienated relationships and for comprehension of the subjectivity and creativity of the working class (Castoriadis, 1979d).

Diverse sociopolitical situations were the scenario and content of these Castoridian reflections. A tentative attempt to establish periods of the history of SouB can be made based on the distinct contextual conditions that the group confronted and the theoretical developments born out of them. Three periods can be differentiated:[8]

a) A first phase from 1949 to 1953 when the group began questioning and distancing itself from the traditional leftist organizations and ideology[9] and reconsidering the revolutionary project. Their opening discussion referred to the bureaucratization and the Stalinization of the revolution, which was the foundational stone of the group's critique during this period. Not only the USSR and the Eastern European realities served as the focus of analysis, other important events such as the start of the Cold War, the Korean War in 1950 and some French strikes that followed the workers' mobilizations of 1947, shaped their reflections. Furthermore, during this first phase, the group centered on discussions about the "organizational question": the structure and the social function of SouB. Different ideas around these topics were discussed among certain members who later would leave the group. Until 1952 the group remained small (they came to be only 12 members) and the publications, small in size, came out infrequently.
b) The second phase was from 1953 to 1960 in which the life of the group was reanimated and new members joined. The death of Stalin, the ending of the Korean War, and the revolts of East Berlin workers in 1953, the Algerian War in 1954, the Hungarian workers' uprising in 1956, and the arrival of de Gaulle to power in 1958 were the main events that moved the group to develop new perspectives and restate certain positions taken in the past. The questions about the political and the social were enriched with notions of self-management (*autogestion*). SouB's publications sold up to 1000 issues and nearly a hundred people from outside attended their public meetings. Nevertheless, in 1958 with the arrival of de Gaulle to power and the newcomers into the group, the organizational question reappeared and ended with the definitive scission of Claude Lefort and Henri Simon.[10]
c) The third period was from the late 1950s to 1965 when more splits occurred and more radical theoretical revisions were made. The

group divided into two at the end of 1959 and the beginning of 1960. Some members, including Castoriadis, were in favor of a more radical rejection of Marx's economic theory and classical positions towards pauperization, economic crisis, the growth of the reserve industrial army and the role of theory, while the rest were in favor of keeping Marxist principles. This discussion lasted for three years as both sides kept disagreeing until their split occurred in 1963. The first group kept *SB* and the rest kept PO. After the split the group published six issues of the review, the last one on June 1965. SB continued functioning until 1966 with a considerable readership: around 1000 copies sold per issue and meetings went up to 200 people. Nevertheless, there was almost no feedback from the members of the group. The work, in Castoriadis' judgment, had become solitary, acquiring a more philosophical character in an attempt to return to the foundations of the conceptions of society and history. Castoriadis proposed then the suspension of the publication.

The three different moments SouB experienced were in response to political and social events that raised a general call to re-elaborate certain aspects of the revolutionary project that had started with the USSR revolution and that appealed to the Marxist theoretical model. As seen, within France there were many political organisms and intellectuals who engaged in this enterprise in one way or another, however, it is arguable that SouB was a unique collectivity that advanced a new political position that sought to maintain revolutionary activity without mystifying theory or a political organism (e.g., "the Party" or "workers" organizations) and at the same time criticizing both capitalism and socialism. As Hastings-King (1999, p. 3) reasonably argues, of all the parties, organizations, and all the media outlets that constituted the French Left, only SouB devised an analytical framework that systematically addressed the implications of bureaucracy, Stalinism, and the emergent socioeconomic order: the implementation of Fordism in France. They not only advanced an alternative of intellectual and political work with shop floor workers, but they also coherently assumed this work with all its consequences at the theoretical and political level.

Reopening the question of society, history, and social transformation, SouB re-elaborated "untouchable truths" about socialism, revolution, and conventional "laws of history and society." Starting from basic questions raised by Marx, SouB was able to reflect on their own beliefs and historical conditions to redefine in an original and unique fashion the socialist and revolutionary project. The political evolution and change suffered by SouB, and especially by Castoriadis, took him to a major philosophical and political elaboration that was original in its context of emergence. Castoriadis, contrary to many contemporaneous progressive intellectuals, maintained a social critique knowing that a revolutionary project included a dimension that involved a perpetual, never fully concluded or achieved elucidation. Nevertheless, the categorical rejection of the idea that there might be a complete theory, and that theory is sovereign, did not assume in Castoriadis' initial activity, the allowance to "say just anything."

Throughout the revision of SouB's different developments during the three phases introduced above, it is possible to track not only the dynamic this group and Castoriadis established with contextual conditions that led their work to develop in the way it did, it also allows us to see how this process of action and abstraction, experienced in different conjunctures, produced the theoretical roots of future conceptions in Castoriadis. Bearing the impossibility of doing an exhaustive history of SouB in mind, the following review of the history of the group intends to focus on main discussions that gave life to the group and led to Castoriadis' main developments.

Le Tambour Café (1949–53)

The discussion raised by SouB in their first publication finds its roots in the political experience Castoriadis had with the Greek Communist Party during 1944/1945.[11] This experience led him to sympathize with Trotskyism and helped to develop his early position toward bureaucracy. Using Trotskyists' last writings as a point of departure, Castoriadis argued that a critical examination of the USSR was essential if Marxist revolutionary theory was to provide a coherent political orientation for militants. Although SouB defended the Trotskyist view in which political organization and ideological "correctness" were fundamental elements of revolutionary politics, they also disagreed with his general conception of Stalinism. Contrary to Trotskyist principles, the group understood bureaucracy not as a direct result of Stalin being in power, but as a phenomenon linked with the Leninist Vanguard Party and its division of intellectual and manual work in revolutionary activities where workers could never transcend mere proletarian consciousness.

For Trotskyists, the Stalinists had lined up on the side of bourgeois order and represented reformism. Trotskyism envisaged a second revolution as the working class rejected Stalinism and re-appropriated the revolutionary core of Marxism. Their tactic consisted in supporting the CP to take power with the hope that it would become fragile and the contradiction between the motivations of the masses for revolution and the real policy of the CP would emerge.

However, at that moment, the events taking place in Eastern Europe demonstrated that the CP in power was not transitory, what led Castoriadis to see bureaucracy as a dominant and exploitative class. Within this perspective, Castoriadis considered reopening the Russian question as a priority. Having this concern in mind, in 1948 Castoriadis and the rest of his comrades that joined SouB published in March 1949 the text: *Socialisme ou Barbarie. An Organ of Critique and Revolutionary Orientation.* Continuing the Marxist analysis of the modern economy and the historical development of the workers' movement, they attempted to respond to new revolutionary challenges, including a new definition of the working class bureaucracy (Castoriadis, 1997n, p. 36).[12]

Initially, the group considered themselves to be Marxists but simultaneously they were open to revising Marxist contents in the light of current socioeconomic and historical conditions. Affirming their Marxist position they wrote:

> Being a Marxist signifies for us situating oneself on the terrain of tradition, posing problems starting at the point Marx and his continuators posed them, maintaining and defending traditional Marxist positions so long as a new examination has not persuaded us that these positions must be abandoned, amending them or replacing them by others that better correspond to subsequent experience and to the needs of the revolutionary movement (Castoriadis, 1997o, p. 37).[13]

This position toward Marxism reflected their understanding of the statement: "Without revolutionary theory, no revolutionary action." For them, theoretical elaboration was inseparable from revolutionary activity. Elaboration neither preceded nor followed revolutionary activity: the former was simultaneous with the latter and each conditioned the other. They did not see theory as the sovereign system of truths given once and for all. Theory for Castoriadis was nothing less and nothing more than a project, a praxis within the ever-uncertain attempt to arrive at an elucidation of the world.

As Castoriadis would argue later on (1988d, p. 29), for the group, praxis aimed at individuals becoming agents for the development of their own autonomy. This praxis, which could exist only as conscious activity, constantly gave rise to new knowledge and theories, given that an exhaustive theory could not exist and only making and doing could make the world speak. Within that understanding of theory, coherent revolutionary theory for

Castoriadis had to start with a comprehensive understanding of capitalism. He introduced the concept of bureaucratic capitalism,[14] which referred to a period of capitalism that followed monopoly capitalism and was characterized by the increasing fusion of the economy and the state. This process of fusion followed a different path in the East and the West, and the USSR was the model for outright state appropriation of the economy, following a process set in motion by Lenin and radicalized by Stalin.

Castoriadis argued that the USSR had nothing to do with socialism but was a type of regime constituted around a total fusion of the bureaucratic party. The Soviet system was the end-state toward which Western bureaucratic capitalism was being borne by the logic of concentration, a new type of capitalism. Soviet capitalism was the furthest extension of the tendencies toward centralization still latent in the more fragmented form, the Western form. However, from the viewpoint of relations of production—an essential point in the analysis for SouB—there was no essential difference from bureaucratic capitalism.

SouB saw the core of the problem in the relations of production in both the capitalist and Soviet systems. The central conflict was given in the bureaucratic capitalist relations of production. For them the Fordist distribution of tasks, and their reconstitution on the basis of a bureaucratic vision of production free of human agents, was irrational because it involved the substitution of a managerial view of the factory for one derived from factory conditions. Fordist production eliminated the creative interaction of workers. The contradiction and source of bureaucratic capitalism's irrationality in the factory emerged at the point of contact between the managerial view of production and actual production. For a rationalized production to take place in a factory, it would need the creative involvement of workers who would enable managers to cope—within a logic of intense rationalization—with the problems that continually changing realities pose to production. The analogy between this conflict at the point of production and the effects of the monopoly-state fusion characteristics of bureaucratic capitalism was clear.

The Russian society was a society of exploitation in which the working-class, deprived of its own working products and expropriated of the direction of its own activity, had the same destiny as if it was under capitalistic conditions. Russian bureaucracy was an exploiting class, which structure, ideology, and modes of economic and political domination of which corresponded to the total concentration of the capital in the hands of the state. The role of this bureaucracy had not only an economic character, but also a political one. It expressed the most profound characteristics of modern capitalist production: the concentration of productive forces, the limitation of private property as the base of the power of the dominant class, the consolidation of bureaucratic corpuses in the big companies and enterprises, fusion of monopolies and the state, and the ruling of economy (Castoriadis, [1949–57] 1979a, pp. 287–305).

For SouB, Russia's economic process took place between two social categories. On one side were the executants, or the proletariat, made up of unskilled workers having only their labor power at their disposal. On the other were the directors: bureaucrats who did not participate in material production and who assumed the management of and control over the work of others.

A bureaucratic state had the same characteristics of imperialism: the merger of economic strength and state power (Castoriadis, 1988e, pp. 51–2). This analysis of bureaucracy and the Russian regime allowed SouB to identify the relations of production as the foundation of the division of society in classes. If traditional private property was eliminated and yet, in spite of that, the workers continued to be exploited, dispossessed, and separated from the means of production, the division within society became the division between managers (or directors) and executants in the process of production. In consequence, the division of contemporary societies into classes in both the East and the West corresponded to the same forms of domination. In Western capitalism and Soviet communism similar phenomena had taken place—concentration of capital, evolution of technique and organization of production, increasing intervention of the state, and evolution of the great working class organizations—leading to similar results: the establishment of a bureaucratic layer in production and in other spheres of social life.

Given that the division of contemporary society was based on those terms, the socialist revolution—in the Castoridian view—could not stop at barring the bosses and "private" property from the means of production, it also had to get rid of the bureaucracy and the influence the latter exerted over the means and the process of production. In order to abolish the division between directors and executants, socialism had to work under the principle of self-management: the complete exercise of power over production and over the entirety of social activities by self-ruling organs of workers' councils.[15] Self-management is what SouB came to understand as socialism, rejecting the dominant leftist focus on who owned the means of production. Socialism meant the self-ruling of the proletarians. In other words, self-government for the working class would require consciousness of itself, its means and its goals (Castoriadis, 1979a, p. 290).

For Castoriadis, in the Russian case, the revolutionary party was responsible for the lack of the proletarian self-management. However, the concentration of economic and political power in the hands of the Bolshevik party that thwarted the attempts of the proletariat to take over the control of the factories, was also a result of the passive proletarian attitude that the party was above the class. In real socialism there should be proletarian management at every level, exercising power without being dominated by the power of the party. The revolutionary organs could not be governmental organisms or bureaucratized worker organizations that established a type of relation with the masses where the directors worked separately from the workers, reducing workers to a passive role where their political action was dominated.

SouB sustained that revolutionary politics of the proletarians should be defined as the activities that coordinated the workers' efforts to destroy the capitalist state. In consequence with this principle, the revolutionary party should be a collective organism that worked according to a historical program implementing the politics of the proletariat. The need for a revolutionary party would only disappear after the world victory of revolution (Castoriadis, 1979e, pp. 103–13).

Even though SouB rejected the Leninist idea of introducing political consciousness into the proletariat through the revolutionary party, still they firmly believed in the need for a revolutionary party. The dilemma that the conditions of the Russian Revolution and the revolutionary party presented to SouB, was the real self-management of the revolutionary organisms and the interests they represented. For the group, the only plausible organism was one that represented the historical interests of the proletarian class based on a proletarian form of organization. However, self-management and its real revolutionary character could not be established as an a priori; it could only be judged and evaluated in daily experience and be modified in its light.

Although SouB was aware that there was no sole right position toward revolution, the group did not acquire an anarchist position. They considered that their basic duty was to promote the workers' interests whose struggle had been kidnapped by the revolutionary bureaucracy. Claiming that they were the only group that could synthesize and integrate the proletarian experience, they declared in 1949 the construction of the revolutionary party as their main responsibility (Castoriadis, 1979e, pp. 117–18).

The discussions the group held in relation to the organizational question—that is, the direction of revolution and the organizations needed for it—brought up what Castoriadis called in 1952 "the profound antinomy" initiated by Marxism. Castoriadis saw a contradiction between the determined revolutionary societal forms defined by Marxism and other possible and unpredictable social organizations that would emerge from the creativity of the masses as it would flourish during and after the revolution. But the groundbreaking character of revolutionary activity resided for Castoriadis precisely in the fact that its content would be original, unforeseeable and, most importantly, a new collective creation that could not be determined by any prescribed program. This would become a major argument in Castoriadis' critique of Marxism.

In any case, as said, SouB believed in the need for a revolutionary party that distanced itself from "fixed" revolutionary programs born out of bureaucratic entities, and that which would take part in bringing about real revolutionary theoretical and practical activities from the proletarian perspective. In other words, SouB should look forward to finding a way to work out revolutionary activities and the antinomic terms it represented. In relation to this issue Castoriadis wrote in 1952:

> The sole theoretical "answer" that can be given consists in saying that the solution of this antinomy [the antinomy contended in Marxist revolutionary activity] will develop during the course of the revolution because the creative activity of the masses is a conscious and rational type of activity, and hence is essentially homogenous with the activity of conscious minorities acting before the revolution begins, but whose unique and irreplaceable contribution consists of an overthrow and a tremendous enlargement of the very content of the historical reason . . . This theoretical "solution" does not prescribe them to us. On the contrary, it tells us that the concrete content of the revolution outstrips every advanced analysis since it consists in the positing of new forms of historical rationality (Castoriadis, 1988f, p. 199).

This position was officially maintained by the group for some years, even though there were discussions in relation to this organizational question, which caused the temporary departure of Claude Lefort.[16] In July 1951, Lefort opposed the construction of a revolutionary party need to construct a revolutionary party because it was too close to a bureaucratic form.[17] In Lefort's perspective, the journal should be an organ of reflection, discussion, and information and not an organization with a programmatic agenda that promoted a discourse of totalities (Molina quotes Lefort (1998, p. 725).[18]

Castoriadis and the majority of the SouB members did not agree on devoting the group's activity only to theoretical discussions or informative issues. For Castoriadis, theoretical, political, and practical tasks were just different forms of the same reality. If the group was to take a position before any problem that affected the proletariat, the group should assume a practical and active position (Castoriadis, 1979d, pp. 131–43). In 1952, they would still state that their principal tasks were the elaboration of a revolutionary ideology, the definition of a revolutionary program, and the promotion of their ideas (Castoriadis, 1988f, p. 205). To meet those purposes, the group had established two main ways of working. Some sessions—held twice a month—were devoted to studying Marx and economic theory, the rest of the sessions—also ordinarily held twice a month—congregated the totality of the members to discuss what were in their opinion the most urgent political problems. Among other topics, they devoted time to discussing workers' unions, the imperialism of the bureaucratic Russia, workers' strikes, and principally, the evolution of the economics and the future development of the bureaucratic capitalism within the two world potencies.

In effect, Castoriadis sought to find political and socioeconomic foundations for his theory of bureaucracy, and at the same time show how it fitted into a historical conception of modern society. For him it was clear that in the East and the West, capital concentration and its interpenetration with the state, as well as the need to exercise control over all sectors of social life—and in particular over the workers—involved the emergence of a new instance of managing production. In this sense, the following evolution of these phenomena in the world-wide sphere, constituted a query that Castoriadis resolved trying to explain how, even though there were strong similarities between the Eastern and Western potencies, their differences would lead to an international conflict.

The group interpreted the Korean War as an event that confirmed the division of the world into two closed zones, within which the system of exploitation had achieved a relative consolidation. They also confirmed the inevitability of war that continued a phase of compartmentalization with localized containment of conflict.[19] SouB sought to identify the deep conflict between U.S. and USSR, by using the word imperialism. As said, to SouB and especially to Castoriadis, both of these were forms of bureaucratic capitalism driven by the general tendencies of capital accumulation and concentration of wealth. The USSR shared those constitutive tendencies still latent in the bureaucratic forms of capitalism: unlimited exploitation, unlimited rationalization, and unlimited terror. In the West, concentration of wealth drove the transition from market-based to monopoly capitalism leading to a final fusion of monopolies with some sectors of the state in the case of the West, or the total state in the Soviet case. Following this logic, the effects of bureaucratic capitalism would produce an interbloc conflict among national and regional monopolies for materials and markets, both foreign and domestic. The group's interpretation of this interbloc conflict led them to pose a possible third world war.[20]

The Korean War not only represented the ultimate form of rivalry between contending states in modern society, it also represented an antagonism between two structural systems, each being a different stage in the concentration of the forces of production. Concentration had gone well beyond the classical monopoly stage and had taken on a different role. In each country, the state had become the backbone of economic and social life.

In SouB's view only a war would be the resolution of differences and similarities between the two potencies in question (Castoriadis, 1988d, pp. 84–5). Castoriadis thought that a new economic crisis for capitalism was inevitable. With Marx's theory of capital and power concentration pushed to its limit[21] and two imperialist super powers left as a result of the Second World War, Castoriadis postulated that a catastrophic war would develop. SouB felt that the Korean War was the confrontation they had predicted, nevertheless, a different reality in 1953 made them change their minds and restate their position toward this issue, recognizing their false interpretation of the events.

To recap: the critique of bureaucracy and the degeneration of the Russian Revolution during this period inspired in Castoriadis the idea of proletarian self-rule. It meant that there was no proletarian consciousness, that the working class could not exercise its power through any delegation, a delegation to a party or any other organism. Throughout this first period Castoriadis sustained the idea of a need for a revolutionary party or organism, although with several restrictions and reinterpretations. Nevertheless, the antinomy that Castoriadis revealed when confronting the organizational question in relation to the revolutionary direction, the real proletarian consciousness and interests, and the role of revolutionary theory led consequently to further questions. This antinomy meant, simultaneously, the need to question prerevolutionary "truths" as well as the traditional conception of the nature, role, and status of theory. This deep interrogation initiated during the winter 1954–5 was enriched by strikes held in France, England, and the U.S., as well as the events in 1956 in Russia, Poland, and Hungary (Castoriadis, 1979b, p. 14).

New perspectives of socialism (1953–5/8)

After 1953 the group started a new phase. It grew in size with new members who helped to reformulate some of the theoretical and practical challenges of the group, as well as notions that had been worked out in the past years. Since 1950 SouB had captivated the interest of some ex-members of the Bordigist Union de Gauches Communistes[22] and in 1952 Jacques Gautrat (Daniel Mothé), Andrée Lyotard, and Pierre and Mirrelle Souyri also became recognized members.

During this phase, the group had distanced itself definitely from Trotskyism given their clear positions toward Marxism, the USSR, their analysis of contemporary capitalism, and their interest in new types of political actions. They became focused on the analysis of new political events that occurred in 1953–6 in Eastern and Western Europe, which animated them to rethink the hierarchy of elements that shaped their conception of the revolutionary project and theory of the proletarian position. Their interpretation of workers' actions and resistance to bureaucratization added to the theoretical interrogations in which they already engaged: the nature of social processes and history; the workers' experiences and their problems; the political problems raised by an international situation changed by Stalin's death; and the possibilities raised by the re-emergence of self-directed political actions.

Several events strongly influenced the group. The uprising of workers in East Berlin[23] during the "June Days" (a general strike in France which shut the country down by paralyzing communications),[24] the Algerian War, and the explosive actions in Poland and Hungary (1954–6)[25] that revealed the crisis affecting the Soviet party, were among the principal ones. For SouB, events in Poland and Hungary indicated a rejection of conventional politics and organizational forms, and the emergence of a new type of revolutionary politics that should be read in light of a new revolutionary theory and concepts of self-management, socialism, and revolution.

SouB was enthusiastic about the new political panorama presented in 1953. They acknowledged their mistake in predicting the Korean War giving two reasons. First, they recognized their overestimation of the independence of the ruling groups vis-à-vis the two blocs' (especially the U.S.'s) own populations. For them the U.S. exercise of power was an artificial phenomenon and not an expression of social contradictions. Secondly, they argued that the cracks in the Russian empire expressed in the East Berlin revolt (1953) played a decisive role in halting the race toward open war.[26] Although still in 1954 they sustained that there was the imminence of a war between the two blocs, they also recognized the slowdown in the race toward war in the attempt of the blocs to stabilize their relations (Castoriadis, 1988h, p. 256).

Moreover, the death of Stalin had contributed greatly to political changes in the international scene, and to the way the USSR was responding to them. In the SouB perspective, the USSR pretended to lessen the Cold War in order to cope with all the crisis manifestations in Germany, Czechoslovakia, Poland, and Hungary, where the bureaucracy had not been able to ensure its power (Castoriadis, 1976a, pp. 139–41).

All these events, including the French workers' manifestations, showed SouB that workers had constructed a relatively clear conception of their organization's interests in opposition to conventional bureaucratic organizations. Workers organized themselves along direct-democratic lines, demanding direct management of production. In this context autonomy[27] became a central element in the SouB lexicon. Workers' actions were interpreted as independent expressions that were linked to a different vision of revolution and socialism.

Socialism came to be understood as direct democracy instituted through worker councils, the aim of which was not just the abolition of exploitation but the institution of social relations that enabled collective influence over society. In consequence, revolutionary theory was to help avant-garde movements understand the connections between experience and self-directed political action, and to see the potential for transformation in a self-reflective way.

When examining how these new elaborations by SouB evolved in their writings, it is interesting to take a closer and more thorough look at the way the group justified their arguments based on events that sparked their reflections, mainly the ones in Poland and Hungary.

In 1952 relations had turned tense between the German building trades and the Party due to a new planned economy schema and the redefinition of wages. Factory workers, construction workers, and miners were in conflict with the government that tried to introduce work quotas and asked them to produce more for less. The East Berlin construction workers began a one-day strike on 16 June, which in part triggered the larger general strike the following day, in which middle class sectors also participated.

After the East Berlin events, a French strike took place in 1953. It gave additional arguments to SouB to back their hypothesis about new workers' expressions that were also taking place in the West. This strike was categorized by SouB as a trade-union betrayal, which demonstrated again the workers' self-organization and the re-appropriation of political spaces of protests. SouB highlighted several crucial points for their analysis of the French strike: the spontaneous character of the strike where no bureaucratic or trade union control had intervened; the strong workers' union that reflected a class unity; the demand for the workers' control over production; and the interpretation of a new form of politics.[28]

The mentioned strikes constituted two different responses to the legitimacy crisis of conventional politics and the bureaucratic organizations that pretended to represent workers' interests. This enabled self-directed workers' actions to control their life and erase the hierarchical structure between managers and workers. Workers founded more democratic ways to organize themselves in councils and deliberative forums through which real socialism could become instituted. This new germ of politics was for Castoriadis the workers' avant-garde to which theory should contribute by comprehending and interpreting the everyday experience of workers at the point of production and its relation to independent political actions.

The following years, 1954–6, new events took place to reinforce SouB's interpretations of 1953 happenings, mainly the Polish crisis and Hungarian revolt. The crisis in Poland that SouB analyzed[29] centered on a series of events beginning with the regained power of Wladyslaw Gomulka in the Polish Communist Party (PZPR) and the clashes in Poznan. The opposition of the USSR to Gomulka, generated by his dislike of the most orthodox and pro-Soviet members, and his desire for a more independent course in foreign policy generated a strong tension in Poland. It was expressed as tens of thousands of Poles took part in pro-Gomulka rallies in Gdansk, Szczecin, and Warsaw on 24 October 1956 (Kramer, 1996). SouB again interpreted this manifestation as the crisis of the bureaucratic regimens in Poland and the Kremlin. SouB considered it a revolutionary movement even though workers' councils were not constituted and real political changes within the party were not achieved. Nevertheless, these revolutionary forces questioned Leninist ideology, gained freedom of expression, and prepared the masses to fight the Soviet military interventions.

SouB saw revolutionary potentiality in this crisis and hoped for an open and crude confrontation between the masses and the Gomulkist party, but it never took place. For SouB the return of Gomullka to power meant the renascence of the bureaucratic tyranny. Politically and economically this party reproduced totalitarian practices. It monopolized authority and did not allow other political organizations to intervene in decision-making processes, especially the Parliament, which was totally controlled by the government (Castoriadis, 1976b, pp. 273–8, 295). In this sense, the Polish crisis was a germ for revolution and another symptom of the crisis of socialism that SouB could add to their list; however, in the eyes of the group it never accomplished the same revolutionary deeds that the Hungarian Revolution did.

The Hungarian Revolution in 1956 was judged by Castoriadis as the first real revolution against bureaucratic systems, the first one that would initiate future revolutions in the East. Contrary to the Polish case where the CP dominated and asphyxiated the movement, the Hungarian workers reassumed their place and voice in society to open up history and create something new through a collective deliberative activity (Castoriadis, 2000a, p. 78).[30]

The Hungarian Uprising began on 23 October 1956 when the working class took on and installed a new government, lasting 18 days before being crushed by Soviet tanks. It began with a students' demonstration to show sympathy for the people of Poland who, that weekend, through Gomulka and the Central Committee of the Polish United Workers Party, had resolutely rebuffed an attempt by a delegation of Soviet leaders who were against them. Students had different demands: elect a new Party leader in a national congress, re-establish friendship with the Soviet Union on the basis of equality, withdraw Soviet troops from Hungary, hold free elections and guarantee freedom for the press (Fryer, 2000, pp. 1–6). Workers soon joined this spontaneous movement. Both factory workers' councils and district-based workers' councils sprang up during the first phase of the 1956 revolution. They demanded self-management of industries, elimination of rules and external impositions over workers, reduction of income inequalities, abolition of control over planning and governmental processes, and implementation of new foreign policies (Castoriadis, 1988g, pp. 57–89). The workers organized a nation-wide political system based on councils, aiming to a direct rule of the producers.

Castoriadis saw in the workers' councils new foundations for different conceptions of political power, economic production, and labor.[31] In his view, they were important because they were fighting for a form of direct democracy and a truthful egalitarian organization, and they vindicated self-management and abolished labor norms imposed from the top. Workers' councils were an effort to abolish the division between directors and those who were being directed, and between representatives and those who were being represented. The Hungarian councils over came the separation between the opposed terms of the technical dimension of work and production, and the political dimension of other spheres of life. They became organizations of self-management and the only legitimate source of decision and expression.

The Hungarian affair served SouB's purposes to confirm their thesis about the emergence of a new phase in the proletarian vision of revolutionary action. It posed again the political question about what a revolutionary movement meant, and how history was not determinant in the course of the social and political forms, as some Marxists argued. The Hungarian Councils were unknown and unpracticed organizational forms in Eastern socialism and Western capitalism. The Hungarian Councils were a manifestation, in a concrete political form, of a new politics, an emerging self-ruling political form in the sense that they established and instituted themselves as the only source of legitimate political decisions and norms that regulated their own collective behavior and life.

In this line of thinking, revolution meant not a state but a process expressed in the self-organization of the people. The form of self-organization established by the councils did not simply mean that people had finally discovered the best form of social organization, but that people had realized that that social form was their own activity of self-organization in accordance with their understanding of their historical situation, and the objectives they posed for themselves (Castoriadis, 2000a, pp. 89–101).

The Hungarian Revolution showed that it was not a problem of knowing the exact content of a revolutionary social form. There was no such a thing as an already given formula of what it would be. The collective and self-governing activity of people was the way to decide what type of revolution they desired instead of having a totalitarian bureaucratic social form. In doing so, the Hungarian Revolution destroyed the mystification of "Stalinist socialism" and posed further questions of what revolution ought to be, what was the role of revolutionary theory, and what it meant to transform the institution of society.

A greater distance between SouB and Marxism became more explicit after their analysis of the 1953 and 1956 events—especially the Hungarian Revolution. Their restatement of concepts such as socialism, revolution, revolutionary activity, and revolutionary theory, led Castoriadis and the group to new interpretations of social change. Through the examination of the content of socialism and revolutionary actions, Castoriadis set the basis for his debate against the determinism and institutions within Marxism and philosophy.

Moved by their urgency to distance themselves politically from the regime of the USSR and its satellites in Eastern Europe, Castoriadis and the group focused on a reflection more inspired by their activism than by an intention to develop a philosophical and anthropological platform to respond to the posed problems. Nevertheless, it is important to note that from the experiences of 1953 and 1956 Castoriadis extracted the raw material for future elaborations in relation to society and history. The incipient notion of autonomy that he started to develop as a shop-floor category emerged from the workers' struggle and their political vindications. It marked a starting point in his later philosophical elaborations in relation to the agency of the subject and social transformation. In the same vein, the problem of revolution and its re-conceptualization emerged from the vindicatory movement in the strikes in the East and the West. They were the germ for the later debate about the deterministic character of history, society, and his concept of creation.

After their work on the Hungarian Revolution, SouB continued a three-part series of texts titled "On the Content of Socialism (I, II, III)."[32] These questioned Marxist principles and economic theory, and emphasized their conception of socialism.[33] They also discussed actions that enabled worker self-management, distancing from Marxism and other political positions held by leftist intellectuals in France. SouB backed these elaborations through a dialogue with the worker avant-garde. The group considered the Renault factory at Billacourt as a representative case to work with when dealing with capitalist labor relations in French Fordism. They were convinced that revolutionary theory should concentrate on the workers' everyday manifestations in order to make explicit connections between them and their protest actions. They sought that their theoretical project should provide analytic tools that would assess new revolutionary challenges. Those resided in creating a schema of self-governing revolutionary action that gave way to a critical social theory. Theory had to grasp and elaborate the potentials of new revolutionary politics interpreting its specific time, content, context, and own problems (Hastings-King, 1999, p. 115).

As seen before, for SouB the emergence of the new revolutionary politics also brought a new emphasis in their re-conceptualization of socialism, a work that Castoriadis and the group continued to develop in 1955–9. In the series of 'On the Content of Socialism' they also approached problems that went from the irrationality present in the organization of production at capitalist factories, to the fundamental division in all contemporary societies: the division between directors and executants.

Concerning workers' management of production within capitalist organization, Castoriadis argued that the real class struggle had its origin in the work in factories. He postulated a permanent conflict between the individual worker and the informally self-organized workers on one hand, and on the other between the production plan and the plan of organization imposed by the company. The alleged capitalist rationalization of work was an absurdity from the point of view of the maximization of production because it excluded the workers from the direction of their own work. In this sense, Castoriadis differed from the Marxist denunciations of the capitalistic factory, which in his view remained superficial. The Marxist view of the rationality of capitalist technique, which prescribed only one type of factory organization, was for Castoriadis an anti revolutionary judgment.

Once again differing with Marx about the true content of socialism, Castoriadis went to argue that socialism was not economic growth nor maximum consumption nor expansion of free time as such; it was the instauration of peoples' control over their activities and work. The program of the socialist revolution and the proletariat's objective could no longer be merely the suppression of private property, the nationalization of the means of production and planning, but, rather, workers' management of the economy and of power (Castoriadis, 1997k, p. 44). The proletariat's objectives could not be achieved by handing over power to a party, however revolutionary and however proletarian this party was at the outset, because this party would inevitably tend to exercise its power on its own behalf and would be used as the nucleus for the crystallization of new ruling group. The realization of socialism on the proletariat's behalf by any party or bureaucracy what so ever was a contradiction in terms; socialism was nothing but the masses' conscious and perpetual self-managerial activity. It was equally obvious that socialism could not be "objectively" inscribed in any law or constitutions, in the nationalization of the means of production, or in planning, nor even in a law instaurating workers' management.

Thus beginning with a critique of bureaucracy, SouB had succeeded in formulating a positive conception of the content of socialism. The proletariat could carry out the socialist revolution only if it acted autonomously, if it found in itself both the will and the consciousness for the necessary transformation of society. Socialism could be neither the fated result of historical developments, a violation of history by a party of supermen, nor still the application of a program derived from a theory that was true in itself. Rather, it was the unleashing of the free creative activity of the oppressed masses. Such an unleashing of free creative activity was possible by historical development, and the action of a party based on this theory could facilitate it to a tremendous degree (Castoriadis, 1997k, pp. 46–8).

In the following years, SouB kept associating socialism with the notion of self-management and direct democracy. They also kept trying to open the notion to other realms of everyday life where socialism should be aiming to give meaning to people's lives and work; to enable their freedom, their creativity, and the most positive aspects of their personality to flourish; and to create organic links between the individual and those around them, and between the group and society. The tasks of revolutionary theory and the function of the revolutionary organization should be appreciated in an entirely new way, understanding that for the worker, the ultimate problem of history was an everyday problem. The real crisis in capitalist organizations (private capitalism in the West and bureaucratic capitalism in the East) was not due to the anarchy of the market or to the falling rate of profit; it was that capitalism was the ultimate negation of autonomy, the negation of people's conscious direction of their own lives. The crisis stemmed from the fact that the system necessarily created a drive toward autonomy, while simultaneously was compelled to suppress it (Castoriadis, 1997l, p. 51).

Socialism should imply the organization of a society transparent to its members, where individuals were able to assume the direction of their life within a decentralized democracy. The only total form of democracy was therefore a direct democracy. This could only be the assumption of power by a federation of workers' councils and the institution of a central assembly that did not presuppose the delegation of popular power but, on the contrary, was an expression of that power.

This type of socialist organization implied then the self-governing action of the working class, the re-appropriation of political spaces that had been usurped by capitalist powers as well as by socialist bureaucracies (Castoriadis, 1997l, pp. 59–70).

"Autogestion": The germ of autonomy (1958–69)

A third phase in the history of SouB began in 1958, a year in which the final split with Claude Lefort took place, and a profound distance among the rest of members of the group started to emerge. During this period, Castoriadis gradually started to focus on his own intellectual project. Without leaving aside his political activism, his interest started to center on the development of his theoretical advances. His political and theoretical divergence with deterministic theoretical perspectives, such as Marxism and structuralism, became strong reasons to refine his framework. As time passed Castoriadis became convinced that the composition and character SouB had acquired produced ineffective political work. This period brought out controversies among the members centered on Castoriadis' more radical questioning of Marxism, in particular, on the direction that the theoretical work was taking, all of which culminated in ending the life of the group.

Different antecedents framed this new phase: the Algerian War, which began in November 1954; the Mollet government (early 1956) that had initiated a partial mobilization in order to send troops to Algeria; the demonstrations by the soldiers that had been called up for the war; the increase of small movements with new demands—especially in 1957 in the factories; and the arrival to power of de Gaulle on 13 May 1958.

In 1954, SouB declared themselves against the French state in the war with Algeria and the French Communist Party (Parti Communiste Français

[PCF])'s alignment with it.[34] However, after the 1954 Algerian affair and the 1956 Hungarian revolution, the next important year for the group was 1958. In this year the inquiry of the organizational question re-emerged. It ended in September of the same year when Lefort and Simon left the group definitively. Nevertheless, although these two losses were significant, between 1958 and 1961 the group grew in number expanding their work into the provinces with students and workers, especially at Renault.

After the split, the work of SouB centered on de Gaulle's actions and on more radical theoretical revisions of Marxist theory. Generally, the group coincided in its reading of Gaullism. It was interpreted as a passage to modern capitalism with attempts to liquidate characteristics of the previous regime, of the French colonialist empire, and of the economic and financial chaos.

In November 1958, when de Gaulle and his constitution were granted approval in a plebiscite, the group saw as evident the need to interpret the overall evolution of modern capitalist countries with different tools other than the ones Marxism offered.[35] Castoriadis deepened in his critiques of the classical Marxist positions on pauperization, economic crises, the growth of the reserve industrial army, the conception of imperialism, and the role and content of theory. This generated another division in the group between the ones that backed Castoriadis' positions, and the ones who were against. Another split occurred in 1963 and more members left the group, Lyotard and Souyri among them. Six more issues of SB (Nos. 35–40) were published after this.

As noted, during this period Castoriadis' work became more centered in his development of foundations for a new conception of society and history, based on his critique of Marxism. He proposed the suspension of the publication in June 1967, because of the sterility of SouB activity within the collective privatization of society (Castoriadis, 1979f, pp. 311–17). Minor activities continued until 1969, when the group finally disappeared.

Even though the work Castoriadis developed after SouB ended is commonly seen as unconnected to this previous period, clearly, SouB laid the foundation for what was to become his more mature philosophical work in the 1970s. Castoriadis' encounter with psychoanalysis in the late 1960s led him to become a practicing psychoanalyst in 1973, influencing his work and changing his routines. This might have caused a different expression of his political militancy; however, his political concerns remained at the center of his reflections.

It can be inferred that after SouB, Castoriadis realized the need to deepen his theoretical analysis in order to address questions raised by his previous work. What Castoriadis had started to envision as an ideal of self-management and the individual's control over the different spheres of life, required more refined theoretical tools to build a coherent theory of society and its subjects that made room for such notions. It included the evident need to contest what he called deterministic inherited ontology—where being is reduced to determinacy—that had hidden the creative character of history, favoring transcendental and absolute principles and social forms (as for example in Marxism). The germ of his project of autonomy born out of SouB—more exactly from his analysis of bureaucracy and capitalism—became consubstantial to his ontology of creation and his elaborations on human imagination and psychical representation. His experience at SouB opened up the question about subjectivity and agency that were necessarily linked to new social forms that implied an examination of democracy and social institutions. This was the core work he started to accomplish from 1970s onward and which began to crystallize in the *Imaginary Institutions of Society*.

Chapter 2

Cornelius Castoriadis' Ontology of Creation

The Imaginary Institution of Society (IIS) is the result of Castoriadis' critique of determinism in theories such as Marxism and structuralism with their functionalist accounts of society and the subject. In this work and in the six volumes of *Les Carrefours du Labyrinthe* he refines his theoretical apparatus to expand this critique. Continuing with the line of thinking that he began developing while working with SouB he advances his reflections on the problem of autonomy and the meaning of revolution and democracy.

This chapter presents the main concepts upon which Castoriadis' ontology of creation is built. By explaining Castoriadis' reinterpretation of the Freudian legacy through his central notion of radical imagination, it is possible to see the way in which a new understanding of subjectivity and agency substantiate his rich notions of imaginary social institutions and autonomy. His anaclisis doctrine, or leaning-on explanation, about the different regions of the self, are also discussed here taking into account the principal critiques of some of his key notions. This interesting and controversial leaning-on explanation shows how, in Castoriadis' view, determinism has to be swept out of any understanding of history and society by bringing in a new conception of creation. The circle of creation illustrated in this chapter shows the way Castoriadis' project of autonomy and its direct relation to democracy involve both individual subjective contents and collective social institutions understood as not totally determined creations of the social-historical.

In *The Imaginary Institution of Society* Castoriadis seeks to avoid the traps of what he calls the two extremes that characterize contemporary theory. On the one hand, he says, there is positivism, scientism, and rationalism; on the other, irrationalism, naïve relativism, and hasty denunciations of science and knowledge. In his view, both positions spring from the belief that thinkers and society will get away from the question of truth, either by resolving it once and for all or by declaring it void of meaning (Castoriadis, [1977] 1984a, p. xiii).

The work Castoriadis develops beginning in the 1970s is an attempt to elucidate the social-historical dimension of society and the imagination that creates societies: the radical imagination and the social instituting imaginary. The social-historical dimension is expressed in society through the imaginary social significations that give life to social institutions and sense to social creations. He explores a new conception of the psychic and social poles of the human being, not by importing reductionist accounts of concepts from other social disciplines, but rather by offering a consistent articulation of different domains of knowledge. He engages philosophy, politics, anthropology, and psychoanalysis, rigorously maintaining the specificity and differentiation of each discipline.

Castoriadis substantiates his ontology of creation with the concept of radical imagination, which he develops by building on Freud's psychoanalytical findings. Castoriadis' use of Freud's work enables him to elucidate not only the nature and character of social institutions but, equally importantly, a new mode of being of the psyche. Castoriadis develops the Freudian understanding of the human unconscious and its theoretical consequences in terms of an undetermined and afunctionalized psyche into the radical imagination. He questions inherited or received ontology and its conception of being, transcending many postulates of Western rationalist philosophical tradition that have defined human beings within rationalist, logical, and deterministic models.

Castoriadis incorporates Freud's contributions to a theory of intersubjectivity that theorizes what Whitebook (1998) calls the privatistic individuality of the subject.[1] While deeply critical of any form of Cartesianism, Castoriadis avoids naïve solipsistic or intersubjective accounts that fail to recognize a human creative dimension. He builds on Freud's study of the unconscious and the human mind's capacity to create via representations of psychical reality, and gives it a new twist that erases the positivist traits and deterministic aspects of Freud's original accounts. Rather than overhauling the Freudian legacy, Castoriadis revisits Freud's original psychoanalytical assertions while overcoming deterministic categories defined within ensemblistic-identitary or ensidic logic. This logic, which structures mathematics and is realized in set theory, is not enough in Castoriadis' view to explain the mode of being of the psyche and social-historical institution. It governs everything that can be constructed and built up by starting with the principles of identity, contradiction, and the excluded third, and organizes anything given by means of univocally defined elements, classes, relations, and properties. It is a determined logic that is nevertheless present in everything humans say or do, and is instituted and sanctioned by society

(Castoriadis, 1987; 1997p, p. 352). In rejecting this structuring and opening up new ones, Castoriadis examines two theoretical problems Freud was not able to elucidate in an appropriate way: the psyche as radical imagination and the social-historical institution as social imaginary.

The Radical Imaginary

Castoriadis builds on Freud's assertion of the main element of the psyche: representation. The Freudian elaboration of the unconscious allows Castoriadis to rework the concept of the psyche as radical imagination,[2] a notion that contests the traditional understanding of the faculty of representation in human beings. Radical imagination is defined as a permanent flux of representation, affect, and intention not subject to determinacy (Castoriadis, 1987, p. 274). It should be understood as the faculty that precedes the distinction between "the real" and "the imaginary" or "the fictitious." Furthermore, it is a necessary precondition for the existence of "reality" as well as the condition for reflective thought for the human being and, therefore, also for the existence of science and even psychoanalysis (Castoriadis, 1997e, p. 133). The radical imagination is one of Castoriadis' main conceptual innovations and is "key in developing his ontology of creation and his understanding of autonomy, which are particularly important in his contribution to social theory.

Castoriadis justifies the term "imagination" by citing its two main connotations: the image in its most general sense, that is, the form, and the idea of invention or creation. He uses the term "radical" to differentiate his concept from what he calls "secondary" imagination, which refers to the most common philosophical formulation: a simple imitative, reproductive, and/or combinatory imagination.

The "Imaginary" in Aristotle and Kant

Castoriadis distinguishes two moments in philosophy preceding Freud where it is possible to identify efforts to define imagination apart from the tradition of the secondary imagination. He credits Aristotle and Kant with the intuition to define "imagination" apart from the shadow of the secondary imagination, though they later fell in line with traditional definitions.

Aristotle's treatise *De Anima* positioned imagination among the potentialities through which the anima judges, categorizes, and perceives an entity. This imagination is closely bound to sensibility or perception; it is a faculty only for beings with sensibility and works on only objects that can be perceived through sensibility. Imagination is not equivalent to sensibility/perception; it is subordinated to it. While the products of sensibility/perception will almost never be "errors," the products of imagination are always "false." Aristotle talked about two manifestations of imagination without making a clear differentiation between them: one related to sensibility/perception, and the other to thinking. The former produces a false and inaccurate copy of the sensible/perceived, and the latter refers to the capacity to evoke images independently of and undetermined by sensibility/perception. This last postulate shows that for Aristotle, imagination was at the base of representing or thinking, that is, the anima can make representations of the world because of the imagination, not because the world can be "implanted" or introduced in the inner subject. However, Aristotle did not profoundly develop this conceptual elaboration, which might have been close to Castoriadis' notion of radical imagination.

Kant, like Aristotle, first related imagination to sensibility/perception. He defined imagination as the faculty of representing an object even without its presence in intuition. This is in the tradition of the "secondary imagination," since it presupposes that the object is already given, that the object has already been formed. Nevertheless, Kant went further when considering the relations between imagination and understanding. He developed the notion of "transcendental imagination," a productive imagination in which the synthesis of reproduction in imagination took place a priori, that is, he conceived imagination as a fundamental power present a priori in human knowledge. However, Castoriadis notes that this conceptual construction became problematic when Kant put sensibility as the empirical perception of sensations (the receptivity of impressions) in opposition to the pure representation of forms (the spontaneity of concepts), leaving imagination between the two. Castoriadis notes that Kant's intuition of the radical imagination in fact became obscured in the second version of the *Critique of Pure Reason*. The latter developments of his thought neglected the foundational role of the imagination favoring instead apperception.

Castoriadis offers two main reasons for the historical omission of the radical imagination. The first has to do with the ontological privilege of the thing (including nonmaterial things) in philosophy, and the second to the direct relation established between that which is thought and that which is true. Ever since the ancient Greeks, thinking has been conceived of as the search for truth, while at the same time it has been related to logos or nous—to the ratio, reason. Opposed to it, doxa, or opinion, has been considered a source of errors or "mistakes" and has been related to the impressions of the senses and/or to the products of imagination. Thus, traditionally, the truth about the world and the self has had to be learned through logos and nous.

With reason given a central position and treated as an unquestionable fundamental, other ontological assumptions followed, such as: "reason can reside in things, ideas or objects, in other words, in substantial individuals, things capable of ideas" (Castoriadis, 1997e, p. 138). The history of philosophy has been devoted to an elaboration of reason as the determining fact of the being, with the human being conceived and approached through rationalist categories. In this sense, the conception of imagination has been under the aegis of reason in the Western production of knowledge and the analysis of empirical reality and its objectification.

As explained later, Castoriadis opposes the rationalist tradition. For him, sensibility and perception are part of imagination. It is imagination that alone gives form and significance to things, which have none in themselves, and it is because of the radical imagination that the subject can give form or significance. It is the subject's faculty of imagination that generates representations from external excitation or internal pressures in the subject, or, to borrow a more precise Fichtean term, from shocks (Antoss) (Castoriadis, 1989, p. 384). The subject exercises a kind of productive imagination through encounters with external objects or information that generates meaning.

Freud and Castoriadis: The foundations of the radical imaginary

To elaborate his conceptualization of imagination, Castoriadis engages with Freud, a third thinker who had an important insight on the radical imagination. Freud's work was constantly centered on the problem of imagination, though he never described it as such in his writings. The treatment he gave to the idea of the "magical omnipotence of thought" or, more generally, to the set of processes described in *The Two Principles of Mental Functioning*, provides good examples.

Throughout his work, Freud referred to the imagination by the term "phantasy," as if he refused to conceptualize it—according to Castoriadis as the constitutive element of the psyche that enables it to create or form phantasies in the psychic apparatus. In a sense it could be said that Freud belonged to the philosophical tradition that subordinated imagination to the objective real, because he always tried to trace the elements of phantasy back to elements of the real.[3] Freud described "phantasy" as derivative of a real experience with authentic material. It is a reproduction of an unconscious combination of things that have been seen or heard previously,[1] that in no way can be thought of or conceived as an original creation. Freud repeated the mistakes of Aristotle and Kant, subordinating imagination to reason. Nevertheless, as we shall see, the Freudian elucidation of the unconscious as having its own logic makes it possible for Castoriadis to re-elaborate his conception of the psyche, particularly the concept of radical imagination, as afunctionalized and not totally determined.

Indetermination and afunctionality in the human psyche

Castoriadis states that Freud demonstrated two important facts with his notion of the unconscious. The first was that psychical representation in humans was neither functional nor totally subordinated to biological substrata. Humans, through the faculty of representation, differ from other living beings, which interact with their environment through canonical, stable, and functional representations, merely responding to the biological functions of conservation and reproduction. The second was that psychical logic cannot be reduced to or conceived only in deterministic logical terms.

Afunctionality of the psyche

Castoriadis examines Freud's *Three Essays on the Theory of Sexuality*, where sexuality is shown as going beyond biological functionality. Through the concepts of bisexuality and the polymorphous perverse, Freud denaturalized human sexuality, showing that for humans there is no fixed or canonical object and aim for the sexual drive. Freud showed that (1) female and male identities are not natural identities with which humans are born and which have a specific behavior and desire attached to them; (2) sexual identity in humans, far from functioning only in the service of species reproduction, is afunctional and not totally subordinated to its biological substrata; and (3) that human sexuality has polymorphous perverse character, in which the psychical valuation of the sexual object (person, thing, or idea toward which the sexual drive is directed) and the sexual aim (the act that would satisfy the drive) do not refer merely to the genital parts of the opposite sex but to any part of the body (Freud, 1962, pp. 2–14). Freud rejected both that everyone is born with her/his sexual instinct attached to a particular sexual object and that individual sexuality is the result of social as well as natural conditions.

The notion of the polymorphous perverse supports Freud's initial statement about denaturalization of human sexuality. Demonstrating how the psychical valuation of the sexual object does not refer merely to the genitalia, but rather to any part of the body, Freud declared a universal disposition to perversion which he defined as sexual activities which either extend, in an anatomical sense, beyond the regions of the body that are designed for sexual union, or linger over the intermediate relations to the sexual object which should normally be traversed rapidly on the path toward the final sexual aim (*ibid.*, p. 16). These theoretical observations raise two conclusions: first, the nature of human sexuality is not reduced to the presumed normal universality of the heterosexual frame and, in consequence, homosexuality cannot be considered a deviation or an abnormal illness in the conventional way.[5] And second, it is possible to choose the sexual object independently from the sex.

As a corollary to his inquiry about sexuality Freud concluded that in human beings there exist both a bisexual nature and perverse polymorphism in love aim and object, which, as said, proved the denaturalized character of human sexuality where there is no fixed or canonical object and aim for the sexual drive. Based on this conclusion, Castoriadis deduces that psychical representation in humans is not functional or totally subordinated to biological substrata; thus it does not respond merely to biological functions of conservation and reproduction.

Indetermination of the psychical representation

The not fully determined character of the psychical representation is re-elaborated by Castoriadis based on Freud's work in *The Interpretation of Dreams*, particularly Freud's conclusions about the basic characteristics and constitution of unconscious representations. Freud interpreted dreams as unconscious manifestations of wish-fulfillment, operating within an associative rather than a deterministic logic. Dreams were governed by at least two mechanisms, condensation and displacement, that demonstrated that unconscious representations are not totally ruled by a deterministic logic.

Freud arrived at the concept of condensation by studying the relationship between the manifest and latent contents of a dream, that is, between the first appearance of the dream in the dreamer's mind and its real significance, the thoughts that are shown through the work of interpretation to lie behind the dream. One of the first conclusions Freud drew was that a dream can be interpreted by analysis because there is no univocal, exact, and precise relation between its original appearance and its meaning.

Freud showed how the latent content is analyzed and becomes understood replacing the manifest content. He first addressed this question by observing how, in the analysis of a dream, various elements may be found to be combined—condensed—into a disparate unity. In other words, images or ideas in the dream can be composite figures containing diverse elements or meanings.

Despite the different ways in which condensation works, what is key for Castoriadis is the concept itself as an essential mode of unconscious functioning. In condensation, a sole idea represents several associative chains that intersect in the idea. Each manifest element is determined by several latent meanings, and each meaning, inversely, may be identified in several elements. For Freud this meant that manifest elements do not stand in the same relationship to each of the meanings from which they derive, and so they do not subsume them after the fashion of a concept (Laplanche and Pontalis, 1993, p. 82).

The condensation phenomenon demonstrates how unconscious representations are not fully determined. The fact that the manifest elements in the dream do not have a specific and determined relationship to each of the meanings from which they derive shows that the principles of what Castoriadis calls ensemblistic-identitary logic do not completely explain the mode of being of unconscious representations. Even though an unconscious representation is a determined phenomenon in psychical life, with wish fulfillment equivalent to unconscious determinism, it still works through undetermined logical relations, as demonstrated in the condensation mechanism. With this, Freud opened the possibility that determinism can operate without the categories of conscious logic or determined relations.

The phenomenon of displacement, explained by Freud first in *The Neuropsychoses of Defense*, corroborated this argument. Explaining hysterical symptoms in a patient, he noticed how an act, or an idea, experience or feeling that is incompatible with the patient's conscience can be separated in the patient's mind into its idea and the affect attached to it. Freud explained that the distressing affect activated a defense mechanism that led the patient to weaken the idea in his/her conscious mind and attach its affect to other ideas that were not in themselves compatible, making a "false connection" that later would be expressed in the hysterical patient (Freud, 1984, pp. 47, 52). What is key for this discussion is that the affective intensity of an idea can be displaced on to other ideas.

Later, Freud presented this phenomenon in *The Interpretation of the Dreams* in the analysis of the "Non-vixit" and "Botanical monograph" dreams. In his analysis of the latter, Freud showed how the essence of the dream thought did not need to be represented by the central elements of the manifest dream, or indeed be in the dream at all, due to the detachability of the idea and its emotional charge. An idea's emphasis, interest, or intensity can be detached from it and passed on to other ideas. He also showed how these ideas could seem to be originally of little intensity but related to the first idea by a chain of associations. Freud named this mechanism "displacement," demonstrating that, as with the condensation mechanism, there is no such a thing as a direct and determined relation between a signifier and its signified in the process of unconscious representation.

The referral structure in the operation of psychical representation was fundamental. Freud continued to develop the concept of association as a theory about the mental apparatus. In order to explain how perceptions are received by the human mind and then linked together in the memory, he stated:

> It is a familiar fact that we retain permanently something more than the mere content of the perceptions which impinge upon the system Pcpt. Our perceptions are linked with one another in our memory—first and foremost according to simultaneity of occurrence. We speak of this fact as "association" (1965, p. 577).

Using the associative mode of psychical operation, he explained the mechanisms of condensation and displacement, demonstrating again that even though in dreams wish fulfillment is a determined phenomenon, psychical logic does not work through determined relations.

For Castoriadis, this possibility that a determined phenomenon could have an undetermined structure is key to the functioning of the psyche and its logic, the products of which cannot be explained or understood only through determined parameters.

Phantasy and radical imagination: Differences between Freud and Castoriadis

Castoriadis relied theoretically on the undetermined nature of unconscious logic initially conceptualized by Freud to demonstrate his own hypothesis about the mode of being of the psyche and its representations, though he differs from Freud in crucial aspects when defining psychical representation. Castoriadis writes:

> The unconscious, Freud wrote, is unaware of time and of contradiction. This dizzying thought, amplified and made even more insistent by Freud's

> entire work, has been almost entirely neglected—when it has not been made to say the opposite of what it states, by transforming the psychical apparatus into a real machinery or by reducing it to a logical structure. The unconscious constitutes a "place" where (identitary) time—as determined by and as itself determining an ordered succession—does not exist, where contraries do not exclude one another; more precisely, where there can be no question of contradictory terms and which, itself, is not really a place since place implies order and distinction. . . . The unconscious exists only as an indissociably representative/affective/intentional flux (1987, p. 274).

This undetermined logic is, for Castoriadis, the result of the being of the psyche, which is itself the genesis of representation, a representation that cannot be dissociated from affect and intention. Analyzing a dream, as a group of representations whose associative path is unavoidable and not determinable, and which is, by implication, characterized by overdetermination[6] demonstrates the creative faculty and the work of the psyche, which instaurates symbolism. The work of the psyche acts as instaurator of quid pro quo: it has the capacity to see in one thing another thing, the capacity to posit that which is not, to see in something that which is not there.

In Castoriadis' view, the dream presents the unconscious representation as it is. Relying on this argument, Castoriadis focuses on analyzing the problem of the psychical representation and what it implies. He notes how:

> In general . . . all "separate" representations that waking logic necessarily distinguishes are certainly formed starting from and in relation to a minute number of archaic representations which *were* the world for the psyche, which have been separated during the long work of the formation of the individual *for the ends of awake existence* and which in turn refer us back to the enigma of an original representing-representation. (1987, p. 276).

Castoriadis' reformulation of psychical representation leads to the main conceptual differences between him and Freud. Castoriadis considers psychical representation—which he names "radical imagination"—to be an immanent condition, faculty or property of the psyche, present before any organization of the drives or any "real" experience, and thanks to which the human being can create his/her individual and social reality. The psyche is creative and exists in and through what it forms and how it forms. Castoriadis writes about representation:

There is no possibility of understanding the problematic of representation if we seek the origin of representation outside of representation itself. The psyche is, to be sure, "the receptivity of impressions," the capacity of being-affected by . . .; but it is also, and more importantly . . . the emergence of representation as an irreducible and unique mode of being and as the organization of something in and through its figuration, its "being put into images." (1987, p. 283).

As mentioned, contrary to this is the Freudian position, which is much closer to a biological determinism and which submitted psychical life to objective reality. Freud structured his theory of the psyche by seeking "real" factors that would account for its history and organization.[7]

This theoretical difference between Castoriadis and Freud rests on the degree to which each author interprets representation as dependent on the biological-corporeal dimension. For Freud the real first announces itself in the psyche through the unpleasant affect of hunger, to which the child responds, drawing the traces of the real by hallucinating the breast in order to re-establish the state of psychic tranquility. For Freud this is the original "phantasmic" representation that becomes the prototype for all further phantasy formation. Against this, Castoriadis argues that the hallucinated breast is a secondary phantasy that presupposes a phantasy-phantasmatization. In other words, the preexistence of the radical imagination in the psyche makes the phantasy possible.

This theoretical difference is manifest in each author's treatment of imagination. Castoriadis argues that imagination takes on a central role in Freud's theory when phantasy becomes an inherent element of the psychic life that operates after the reality principle has been established. With the introduction of the reality principle, a different kind of thought activity is separated from the experience of reality within the psyche and which remains subordinated to the pleasure principle. Freud explained the origin of these representations, as well as the reasons why they do not produce scenes of biologically canonical satisfaction, by first considering possible answers such as the "real" origin for the pleasing representation, and thereafter deriving phantasies from certain phylogenetically constituted original phantasies. This, Castoriadis believes, was how Freud uncovered the creative character of imagination.

The differences between Castoriadis and Freud as they conceptualize imagination (phantasy) and representation have significant ontological consequences. Through establishing these differences with Freud, Castoriadis is able to build his concept of radical imagination and set the basis for what he calls a new ontology of creation. In order to develop his ontology Castoriadis relies once again on his elaborations of the mode of being of the unconscious and theorizes a new way of thinking where what is determined and measurable is thought and conceived in and simultaneously with indeterminacy. To support this original view Castoriadis poses the concept of a magmatic logic, without, however, denying the always present ensidic logic, asserting that the world includes within itself a dimension that not only lends itself to (is compatible with) an ensidic organization, but corresponds to such an organization. To be sure, the world indefinitely lends itself to ensidic organizations but cannot be exhausted in them, leaving room for a simultaneous magmatic mode of being that entails a different logic (Castoriadis, 1997c, p. 364).

Castoriadis defines magma as a sui generis mode of organization belonging to a nonensemblist diversity, a mode of coexistence with an organization that contains fragments of multiple logical organizations but which is not reducible to a logical organization. A magma contains sets but it is not reducible to a set or the sum of its parts (Castoriadis, 1997g, p. 12). This neologism refers to a mode of being that is essentially indeterminate and that rules out the possibility of total determinacy. It is neither structured as such into distinct, identical items and finite mutual relations, nor it is completely chaotic or shapeless. It has a dimension that lends itself to the possibility of structuring it into identical elements and their sets, in other words, "A magma is that from which one can extract (or in which one can construct) an indefinite number of ensemblist organizations but which can never be reconstituted (ideally) by a (finite or infinite) ensemblist composition of these organizations." (Castoriadis, 1987, p. 434). It is possible to understand a magma by thinking of a multiplicity which is not one in the received sense of the term but which we mark out as such; and which is not a multiplicity in the sense that we could actually or virtually enumerate what it contains, but in which it is possible to mark out in each case terms that are not absolutely jumbled together.

Magmatic logic becomes pivotal for Castoriadis' ontology of creation as it conceptualizes a mode of being not totally subjected to determinacy. It tackles the unavoidable and ever present indeterminate character, not only of psychical representation and the human unconscious, but of the totality of the existing-being, the ontological condition of which is not completely determined despite its ensidic dimension. For Castoriadis everything that is and everything that is conceivable is a magma (Castoriadis, 1997j, p. 299).

In sum, Castoriadis reworks Freudian psychoanalytical insights to propose new foundational concepts such as radical imaginary and magma, while seeking to question the inherited deterministic ontology that has infused Western thought—from Plato to the present—where every thing that is, is determined. By giving a new ontological status to the radical imagination, Castoriadis opens up a whole new perspective on Being, where rationalist essences are contested and creation is what defines our nature, history, and social institutions. Based on the concept of the radical imaginary Castoriadis accounts for the totality of the existing-being, explaining how we become humans within a circle of creation.

The Existing-Being

It is only through radical imagination that humans become social beings who relate to the nonsocial. Even though when theorizing the radical imagination Castoriadis distances himself from biological determinism, he never neglects the strong ties between the human psyche and physical, biological, corporeal reality, or other regions of the self. Castoriadis conceptualizes the totality of the existing-being with its different strata or regions through a leaning-on relationship. In Castoriadis' ontology, the existing-being comprises the strata of the physical or natural, the living-being, the psychical, the social-individual, the social-historic, and the individual and collective autonomy. Castoriadis postulates these strata as heterogeneous and irreducible to each other, but each as necessary to enable the emergence of the others as a completely new creation: each leaned on the one that came before. The terms "heterogeneous" and "irreducible" have to be understood in the light of Castoriadis' concept of creation, where a creation is conceived as a completely new thing whose existence was neither predetermined by nor was a logical consequence of the existence of another stratum. However, the existence of one stratum enables the existence of the next, which emerges as a creation ex nihilo—which implies neither creation cum nihilo (without means and conditions) or in nihilo (without any point of reference). The creation leans on what is given, is conditioned and limited by it, but is not determined by it. (Castoriadis, 1983; 1993c, p. 5).

In breaking with the traditional philosophical determinist view, Castoriadis formulates the leaning-on explanation or account of creation not as a linear process or a sequence of inevitable and progressive consequences. Instead, each stratum emerges as a new creation that is neither a logical consequence nor a result with a specific aim. Each stratum can be defined as a "for-itself", meaning that each forms its own world, satisfying its own goals through auto-reference and closed auto-reflexive patterns. A "for-itself" creates its own closed world in creating itself, and vice versa. A "for-itself" has the capacity of self-alteration and has three essential faculties without which it would not exist as a living being: intention of conservation and reproduction; affect referred to pleasure/displeasure or attraction/repulsion; and representation. Representation here does not mean a perfect copy of the external world, but the presentation through which the living being creates its own world, starting from what are mere external shocks (Castoriadis, 1992, p. 16).

Castoriadis describes the multiplicity of regions or strata of the being as follows:

(a) The living-being. Every living being, from the single cellular level on to the most complex organism, can be considered as a "for-itself". The living-being involves therefore a natural and biological dimension.

As a "for-itself", the living being cannot represent itself out of its own interior. A "for-itself" cannot be conceived except from within. It exists in and through a permanent closure. However, its closure does not mean that there is nothing "outside"; certainly there is. The "for-itself" encounters the external through what Castoriadis calls a shock. In Castoriadis' view, nature does not contain information waiting to be gathered, it only announces its presence through a shock that does not mean information in the strict sense. The "for-itself" encounters the external, which becomes something only as the for-itself forms it. This can be called the cognitive function of the living being.

(b) The human psyche. The human psyche is not defined by Castoriadis as a homogenous whole, but as a plurality that contains various intra-psychical "instances" or "psychical persons." It refers in psychoanalytical terms to the ego, id, and the super-ego.

The specificity of the human psyche consists in its defunctionalization in relation to its biological component. In other words, the human psyche does not follow functional canonic patterns that respond to biological functions. It is in the human psyche where the radical imagination and its quid pro quo faculty operate, enabling unfixed representations and noncanonical responses, entailing the predominance of representational pleasure over organ pleasure.[8] The human psyche experiences a stratification process, from a closed monad to a social individual, as briefly explained later.

(c) The social individual. This is the individual understood as a social product. It is the transformation of the human psyche by society. Society produces social subjects by providing sense, meaning, or signification to the human psyche. As already said, both society and psyche are irreducible, but also indissociable: society must provide social sense in order for the psyche to survive; the psyche cannot live unless it is socialized. To be sure, individuals are made by society (Castoriadis, 1991c, p. 61).

(d) The society or social-historical. Society is created by what Castoriadis calls an anonymous human collective. It is a creation that no other order can accomplish. The social-historical has two poles: the human psyche and society. The human psyche is asocial; it is not predestined by nature to be socialized. However, it becomes socialized through the imposition of society. It is the social-historical that makes it possible for a society to stay together and reproduce itself throughout time. This amounts to saying that the human being is a creation, that it creates itself through society and vice versa.

(e) The individual and collective autonomy. Autonomy is only possible through self-reflection, deliberate self-government, and self-transformation in both the individual psyche and society. As a social individual, the autonomous subject can become so only through social institutions that foster and enable autonomy. This is not to say that such institutions "come first" or that they necessarily produce autonomous subjects. Autonomous subjects and institutions are interdependent, however, as discussed later, neither individual nor collective autonomy is a finished stage or specific state. Autonomy refers to an endless process by which both individuals and society are put into question before themselves and are able to create new social forms and new and different subjectivities.

Castoriadis develops in more detail his explanation about the totality of the existing being using the anlage or "leaning on" explanation, discussing properties and processes taken place in the different strata mentioned.[9] However, even though it is not possible to think about the human subject and society while ignoring any of these strata, I am focusing on processes that directly deal with the human subject from the inception of its psyche into society to its forms of autonomy.

According to the anlage or "leaning on" explanation, the subject is a social product, it cannot exist outside society. In order for the individual to become a subject, its psyche must come into the social institutions through an imposed and "unnatural" stratification process and become socialized. Once again, Castoriadis follows Freudian conclusions that are reinterpreted under new and different theoretical principles.

The stratification of human psyche

Castoriadis responds to the question: "how do we become humans?" by using the leaning-on explanation, where different regions or strata of the being emerge as new creations that do not follow an entirely predetermined logic or program. In the case of the human psyche, this means that it is not "naturally ordained" to become social. Nevertheless, through a process of stratification the human psyche has to "enter" society or risk dying. And even though the psyche never gives up its private world entirely, society will impose itself on it through subsequent stages to which I will only succinctly refer here.[10]

From birth the human psyche suffers a process of stratification, undergoing several stages. This stratification begins as a closed monad that bursts apart during a triadic phase and passes through an Oedipal stage, ending as a social individual. This occurs through the sublimation process, which can only take place by means of essential conditions that are rigorously external to it. Sublimation is the taking up of psychical forms that are socially instituted or, in other words, it is the appropriation of the social by the psyche through the constitution of an interface between its private world and the public or common world. By means of sublimation, the psyche will reshape its own drives based on social contents (Castoriadis, 1992, p. 8).

The monadic stage is characterized as an autistic one.[11] Here, the subject can only refer to itself, and is unable to posit a distinction with respect to itself and everything else. There is no way of separating representation from perception or sensation. The baby identifies itself as the breast, establishing no differentiation between itself and the mother (or her substitute). The baby experiences itself as omnipotent, in the sense that it is the only source to satisfy its needs, the only source of pleasure. This is the nature of the initial psychical monad, which is closed upon itself, absolutely egocentric, and all-powerful, and which lives in the felt experience of the original identity in which I=pleasure=meaning=everything=being. This experience impinges on the human psyche in a way that the phantasy-scene attempts to reproduce it as best it can, whenever it is possible. When this state of autism is broken by the presence of the "other" and separate objects, the subject responds by trying to reconstitute this initial world interminably in phantasies.

Once the psyche has broken up its monadic stage, it will be forever thrown off-center in relation to itself: "oriented in terms of that which it is no longer . . . *the psyche is its own lost object*" (Castoriadis, 1987, pp. 296–7). But even though this aim reigns in the fullest and most intractable manner over the unconscious process, the psyche must accept this imposition—though not completely—in order to be included in the world.

The following phase is the triadic phase that begins as the monad is broken by the imposition of the other (otherness) on the subject. This occurs through a series of breaks inflicted on the psychical monad, by means of which the social individual is constructed as divided between the monadic pole[12] and the series of external constructions imposed on it. The successive formations of the subject, which must gradually extend, take into account both the separation and the diversity imposed on the psyche, and which exist only as attempts to hold this diversity together. These different restructuring phases cannot be seen as developmental stages. They imply that the psyche must be continually restructured around the monad nucleus. Thus, there are multiple instances in the human psyche that coexist in conflict, though not in total opposition. In the psychical apparatus there will be a tendency toward closure of each instance, but at the same time a relative opening of that closure. It is this mode of the psyche being in flux that Castoriadis referred as magmatic.

During the triadic phase the psyche has to give up its original omnipotence in order to "accept" the other. Initially, the baby can only grasp the other by means of the sole schema available: the monadic schema of omnipotence. In consequence, the image of the other that gets constituted this way is, therefore, the projection of the baby's own image of itself. In the triadic phase the baby's early imaginary omnipotence over the breast is forcibly displaced by the other—by the breast that turns out to be sometimes unavailable. The baby then projects onto the other the imaginary schema of omnipotence and establishes the fundamental pattern of phantasy that includes the subject, the object, and the other. This triadic phase represents only the first step in the psyche's socialization, in the sense that the psyche gives up its omnipotence. However, socialization is only relative because omnipotence is simply projected onto the other. The psyche keeps this imaginary other within its grasp, continuing to control the other through its wishes in phantasy (Castoriadis, 1983, pp. 305–9).

It is not until the Oedipal phase that the child must confront a state of affairs that can no longer be manipulated at will. It is at this stage that the child has to accept the existence of an external, noncontrollable "reality" and is faced with the need to join the social world that is being imposed. The other—the mother or its substitute—strips herself of her omnipotence by referring herself to a third party, signifying to the child that her desire has a different object than the child itself, and furthermore that she is the object of the father's desire. By including a third party, the mother cedes omnipotence to it. This third party will in turn signify to the child that no one is absolutely omnipotent. It is through this movement that the child is forced to recognize the other, and human others, as subjects of autonomous desire who can interrelate with one another independently of his or her will. Through this understanding the child is then referred to society as such, to the collective social institution of signification (*Ibid.*). The Oedipal stage sets before the child the unavoidable fact of the social institution as the ground of signification, making the child realize that signification does not depend uniquely on any particular person. It is in this way that the child is able to accomplish the sublimation process, which is nothing more than becoming socialized within the imaginary institution of his/her own society.

The monad/monadic stage as a main phase in the psychical stratification process posed by Castoriadis has been much debated. Whitebook's (1995, pp. 177, 196, 197) main criticism referred to the tension existing between the monadic and the social-historical. Whitebook found the radical heterogeneity that Castoriadis postulates between these two theoretically inconsistent. For Whitebook it is necessary to find a disposition in the psychical monad that enables its access to the social order without implying a violent imposition over the psyche. In Whitebook's view, Castoriadis has drawn the productive power of imagination so strongly that he cannot elucidate the monad breakup. From this argument, other theoretical faults derive. A direct consequence is that Castoriadis cannot ultimately avoid a psychoanalytically formulated version of subjective idealism. That is, if the psyche produces everything out of itself, there would be no way in which it could meet anything different from itself and its own products. And additionally, in a certain way, Castoriadis falls into the same line of thinking of Kant. Given his lack of explanation of how the psyche lends itself to socialization, "the fit between psyche and society rests on no more than a 'lucky' accident" (Whitebook, 1995, p. 197).

These criticisms ignore Castoriadis' leaning-on explanation and the way he elucidates the relations among different strata in the circle of creation. The idea of leaning-on contests traditional deterministic relations established between psyche/soma and psyche/society. The concept of creation defines the new emergence of one stratum from another, irreducible but indissociable. As a creation a stratum is something entirely new that does not emerge as a reflection of a previous instance, or as a reproductive transformation or simple combination of elements present in a preceding stage.

Being is creation, what Castoriadis calls a *vis formandi*[13] or force of formation that is never completely embedded or exhausted in a determinate set of forms. Undetermined creation, however, does not mean unconditioned, detached, or without constraints and relations. Creation in the strict sense poses new laws that are conditioned but which are a-causal and are not entirely determined. In other words, it refers to a faculty of making be, of bringing out of a "for-itself", new modes of being, determinations, and laws that will henceforth be that self's laws, determinations, and modes of being.

Castoriadis writes:
> under certain conditions the "inorganic" can produce the "organic": the living being brings about the appearance of laws and qualities that, as such, have no meaning in the physical realm. It is immediately evident that the emergence of the being-for-itself (the living being, psyche, the social-historical) entails an essential fragmentation of total Being/being . . . The fact of creation also has weighty ontological implication . . . it entails the abandonment of the hyper category of determinacy as absolute . . . but it is a logical error to think . . . that due to this fact one must replace this hyper category by the idea of absolute and complete indetermination. My philosophy is not a "philosophy of indetermination." Creation means, precisely, the positing of new determinations—the emergence of new forms, eide, therefore ipso facto the emergence of new laws—the laws appertaining to these modes of being. At the most general level, the idea of creation implies indetermination uniquely only in the following sense: the totality of what is never so totally and exhaustively "determined" that might exclude (render impossible) the surging forth of new determinations (1997c, pp. 368–9).

Castoriadis adds:

> What is this "self" that makes itself be, without "yet" being a determinate something, but which is going to determine itself thus and not otherwise? This is what I call the groundless, the Chaos, the Abyss of the (singular or collective) human being (*ibid.*, p. 404).

Creation presupposes the chaos from which it emerges; it emerges to cover that chaos that nevertheless manifests itself in and through such an emergence by continuing to be the source of its permanent alterations. This is what the circle of creation is about, it cannot account for an origin, foundation or cause other than itself, which is its own origin. It does not pose any kind of opposition between strata that would not permit new creation. The emergence of the living-being makes evident the irreducible character between the physical and the living-being strata, where a Hegelian synthesis is not possible, not thinkable. Strata cannot be cut or separated as distinct units, as in the case for example, of the physical and the biological, which are irreducible but which in the totality of existing-being cannot be thought or conceived separately. Creation nonetheless presupposes union and tension in the new emergence of alterity, a differentiation and heterogeneity that makes itself other than itself.

Understanding being as creation provides a new way to theorize the tension between psyche and society. The social fabricates individuals, and individuals are nothing but society. Castoriadis does not postulate an absolute polarity between the individual and society, but a polarity between psyche and society that is dynamic. He does not postulate a contradiction between antithetical pairs through which synthesis will produce a new thing. Oppositions are conceived simultaneously, and one element refers to the other in a circle of creation. The new creations, the new emergences, are not consequences, but rather new strata of the existing-being, radically different and irreducible to the previous ones. Castoriadis answered the question: can the same produce a completely different "other," by establishing a difference between the new understood as a consequence (any possible combination of previous elements) and the new as a real other, an alterity. Creation, as Ciaramelli (1997, p. 45) correctly puts it, is a matter of thinking, as the very advent of Being, the movement of an original self-presupposition whereby *what is* surges forth starting from an alteration of itself and therefore proceeds from a "self" that is not *yet* what it is going to become.

Creation does not necessarily proceed from something else and does not have its origin somewhere else, it has within itself precisely the ontological energy to detach itself from itself and to exist as origin. In this sense, the ontological genesis is to be elucidated as creation.

Specifically referring to the relation of psyche to society, Castoriadis writes:

> [The psyche] at all its stages carries the traces of its point of origin, of an initial state in which subject, world, affect, intention, connection, meaning are the same. The social individual, as society produces him, is inconceivable "without the unconscious"; the institution of society, which is indissociable from the institution of the social individual, is the imposition on the psyche of an organization which is essentially heterogeneous with it—but it too, in its turn, "*leans on*" the being of the psyche (and here again the term "leaning-on" takes on a different content) and must, unavoidably, "take it into account" (1987, p. 298).

Psyche and society cannot be thought of separately. It is not a matter of establishing immanent potentialities in the psyche, or a mediation between the two. Rather the individual is social, a fragment as it is each time instituted (Castoriadis, 1997c, p. 377).

The psyche is in no way predestined by nature to society, as Castoriadis writes, making reference to the Aristotelian postulate about the psyche existing only as "form" or "entelechy":

> The psyche is a form in so far as it is forming, ... the "entelechy" in question here is something entirely different from the predetermined predestination in view of an end, a definite *telos*... this "entelechy" is the radical imagination, *phantasia* subjected to no given end but the creation of its ends, ... the living body is the human living body in so far as it represents and represents itself, ... it puts things and itself into "images" far beyond what would be required or implied by its "nature" as living being. For the living human body, that is to say, originally, for the psychical monad, all external calls, all external or internal "sensorial stimulations," all "impressions" become *representations* (1987, pp. 300–1).

Society, the culture phenomenon, cannot be considered a predetermined telos for the psyche. To sustain the contrary would be to deny the existence of radical imagination and its ontological status.

This argument also indicates how Castoriadis is not sustaining the Kantian postulate in relation to "the lucky accident." It is through representation that the human being has access to the world tout court. This does not mean that for Castoriadis nothing else exists but representation. It was Kant who shifted out the a priori condition of experience, who believed it was solely on the side of the subject, forgetting that there are also conditions of experience on the side of the "object," and placed everything under the sign of necessity. In Castoriadis' view, there is no sense in claiming to be able to bring the ultimate facts under any sort of "necessity," nor in calling "accident" that which is near or far from the contingent and the necessary, within which alone the contingent and the necessary are effectively actual and thinkable (Castoriadis, 1997c, p. 366).

In Castoriadis' theory, psyche and society are mutually constitutive and, thanks to the radical imagination and its representational capacity, both can be fabricated as socio-historical products. The way Castoriadis theorizes this aspect reflects the originality of his work, where, as discussed later in greater depth, notions such as the social-historical and the imaginary instituted/instituting power come into his theoretical framework to

. theory of creation of society, its reproduction, its closure, and tory potentiality.

The Social-Historical as the Anonymous Collective's Creation

Psyche and society

Summing up an important conclusion of the previous section, it is clear that Castoridian theory does not take the subject simply as a "real" entity or as an absolute given. The subject has to be "made," it is a social and historical creation that becomes possible thanks to the socialization and sublimation processes that the neonate has to confront. Society, in the leaning-on theory, is a necessary stratum for the subject to survive, and for the psyche to find the required sense for its functioning. Castoriadis writes:

> . . . there must be a society in existence, so that these inept and insane beings [neonate humans] can survive and become human, and there is nothing in the human unconscious capable of producing the basic characteristics of every society, that is, institutions and imaginary significations. The psyche cannot be reduced to society, even if the socialized subject is almost nothing but successive layers of socialization, but the psyche as such, in its depth, cannot be reduced or confined to society and society cannot be confined to the psyche because, yet again, there is nothing within the human unconscious that can produce institutions. . . . The only thing one can say is that there must be some sort of correspondence between the demands of the psyche and the demands of society. This correspondence is reduced to the fact that institutions and social imaginary significations must offer meaning to the socializable psyche; that is, they must create for the psyche a daily world where . . . distinctive human beings exist, where all these are combined and intertwined, and where, for the socializable subject itself, life and even death have a meaning (2010a, p. 156).

Despite the fact that society works on the individual psyche to produce the subject, society is not merely the sum of individual psyches. Society is the product of an anonymous collective and its instituting imaginary. What the radical imagination is for the singular psyche, the social instituting imaginary is for society. The latter is the social dimension of the former.

Together, working in their indissociable and irreducible relation, they create individuals and society.[14] For Castoriadis it is impossible to conceive society out of the psyche alone, because the unconscious does not produce social institutions by itself.

This creative circle where imaginaries are at work gives rise to the imaginary social significations (ISS) and social institutions. ISS are defined as creations of worlds of sense and significations that emerge from the radical imagination and the human collective imaginary (Castoriadis, 1983, p. 353). These impose social ways of being on the individual psyche by providing sense to the subject and validating him/her as a social being.

ISS constitute the web of meanings that permeate, orient, and direct the whole life of the society, keeping its unity and internal cohesion. They give society norms, values, language, tools, procedures, and methods of doing and dealing with the world. These constitute a network of significations called "a magma of ISS" that is embodied in the institution of a given society (Castoriadis, 1997g, p. 7). This magma establishes what is real and what is not, what is meaningful and what is meaningless; it defines what the concepts of society, man, woman, child, etc, are in a specific society. It answers questions raised by every society: "Who are we as a collectivity? What are we for one another? Where and in what are we? What do we want? What are we lacking?" (Castoriadis, 1987, pp. 146–147).

Only relative to this magma of significations is it possible to understand the choice of symbolism made by any society—in particular, the choice of its institutional symbolism—as well as the ends to which it subordinates "functionality" (Castoriadis, 1997g, p. 7). ISS give life, meaning, and identity to social institutions, which can be defined as sanctioned symbolic networks working among human collectives. ISS make social institutions into "efficient apparatus," combining functional and imaginary components in variable proportions and relations. However, neither ISS nor social institutions can be conceived as systems that are solely functional, integrated series of arrangements geared to satisfying the needs of society, nor merely as intellectual constructs. They go together with the creation of a drive for the society, a global intention, affect or a cluster of affects, permeating the whole of social life (Castoriadis, 1997r, p. 336).

ISS do not exist strictly speaking in the mode of representation; they are of a different nature. Comparatively, they are larger than any individual phantasy and have no precise place of existence. They can be grasped only indirectly and obliquely, since they denote nothing while connoting just about everything. Castoriadis describes the social as intangible, fluid, changeable, detached:

The social is what is everyone and what is no one, what is never absent and almost never present as such, a non-being that is more real than any being, that in which we are wholly immersed yet which we can never apprehend "in person." The social is an indefinite dimension, even if it is walled in at every instant—a definite structure and at the same time one that changes, an objectifiable articulation of individual categories and that which, beyond all articulations, sustains their unity (Castoriadis, 1987, pp. 111–12).

Through the work of the social imaginary, the social means simultaneously creation, permanence, alteration, and destruction of social institutions. The social as instituted always presupposes the social as instituting, something capable of changing what is instituted and sanctioned by a collectivity, and capable of bringing new forms into being in order to exist "within" them. The social-historical does not create, once and for all, a new ontological type of order characteristic of the genus society. This type is each time materialized through different forms, each of which embodies a creation, a new eidos of society. This creation, understood as the work of the social imaginary, of the instituting society, is the mode of being of the social-historical field. Society is self-creation deployed as history (Castoriadis, 1993c, pp. 5–7).

If there were not always emergence or creation of ISS or social institutions, history would be the constant repetition of the same. "History would be impossible or inconceivable outside of the productive or creative imagination . . . as this is manifested and indissoluble in both historical doing and in the constitution, before any explicit rationality, of a universe of significations" (Castoriadis, 1987, p. 146). The same counts for cultural diversity since ISS and social institutions can, through the ongoing process of socialization, produce different social forms and cultural differences.

What makes it possible for the ISS to function in the social real is what Castoriadis called legein and teukhein. Society institutes itself as legein—saying, language, systems of meaning—and teukhein—making, ordered practice, social organization. Teukhein is the identitary dimension (which can be termed functional or instrumental) of social activity; legein is the identitary dimension of social representing/saying, which presents itself in particular in language in as much as language is also always necessarily a code, even though both lean on the identitary dimension they are already, as such, social institutions where magmatic logic is also present.

The operations of legein and teukhein are necessary for instituting society and the realization of its stability. They bring instituted society into existence.

Without the instituted moment of stability there cannot be a human world; legein and teukhein together produce the necessary "rational adequacy" of what emerges from the intrinsic and inherent magmatic substratum of society.

In effect, the ISS of any society can be instituted because they rely simultaneously on both ensidic and magmatic logic. Despite the magmatic noncountable and ever-changing character of the ISS, as well as their ambiguous mode of being with widely spread referrals, ISS are amenable to organizing operations and structured orders. The fact that a magmatic way of being cannot be fully reconstituted from an identitary/ensemblist order by retracing backward the extracted/constructing steps that were taken to generate it, as well as the fact that it cannot be reconstructed "analytically," that is, by means of set-theoretical categories and operations, does not mean complete chaos. The social world takes into account that the operations of identitary/ensemblist logics also represent a reduction and an imposition into its noncountable magmatic ambiguity.

In sum, society institutes itself as both ambiguous and certain, changeable and stable, unpredictable and predictable; it institutes itself at once in magmatic and ensidic dimensions, carrying both dimensions in itself, even though its most apparent way of behaving reflects and responds to its reproduction need, that is, the closure and fixation of its ISS and institutions.

Social Closure and Autonomy

Society establishes and creates a world of auto-reference. The "self" of the society, the instituted imaginary, seeks protection against transgressive tendencies of the radical imaginary. It perceives any attack on itself as a mortal threat to its identity. For this reason, society tends to close in upon itself. Society as such, as do its socialized individuals, operates within a representative and cognitive closure, representing and signifying its world through the contents given by ISS. It is the way a society guarantees its learned mode of being as well as the permanency of its institutions. Up to some point, society must produce individuals that ensure its reproduction by canceling any type of transgressive interrogation. This is what Castoriadis calls closure.[15]

In any closed society, any question that its language can formulate must also be answerable within the magma of its ISS. This entails that questions concerning the validity of the social institutions and the significations cannot be posed. The exclusion of such questioning is ensured by the establishment of a transcendent, extra-social source of institutions and significations, such as religion.

In this way, societies institute themselves in and through the closure of meaning, becoming heteronomous. They avoid calling into question their own institutions and they produce conforming individuals for whom interrogating the law is not merely forbidden but inconceivable and psychically unbearable (Castoriadis, 1997d, p. 86). Heteronomy contains or presupposes a unitary ontology that is consubstantial with the postulate of the homogeneity of being. The homogeneity of society, which from the point of view of signification should not be interrupted, is one consequence of the unlimited exigency of signification as a response to chaos. Such a response entails the positioning of an extra source for the institution (and for signification) and therefore, the occultation of the self-institution of society, the covering over by humanity of its own being as self-creation. Misrecognition by society allows it to posit its institution out of reach, escaping its own action. This amounts to saying that it allows society to instaurate itself as a heteronomous society in a cleavage, itself henceforth instituted, between instituting society and instituted society, in the covering over of the fact that the institution of society is self-institution, or self-creation. "In positing its institution as something imposed on it by a source external to itself, society covers over the Chaos, or establishes a compromise with it; it defends itself against the Abyss that it is in itself" (Castoriadis, 1997n, p. 338).

Nevertheless, even though society institutes itself as heteronomous, heteronomy is neither structural nor determinant/determining in society. The fact that a society would affirm its own inalterability in order to stabilize itself does not mean that society is not already a creation. It creates itself as a heteronomous society, it moves within the circle of already accomplished creation (Castoriadis, 1997h, p. 318).

Explaining this relation between the closure and the openness that is present in every society, Castoriadis elaborates on autonomy as the condition that opposes heteronomy. In IIS, Castoriadis presents this concept as a reworking and refinement of his early concept of autonomy elaborated in SouB. Expanding on what he had proposed earlier in relation to auto-management and worker's self-direction, he engages psychoanalysis to incorporate it into his ontology of creation.

Here autonomy is defined as the break of the closure and heteronomy of society, which Castoriadis illustrates with the example of ancient Greeks' invention of democracy and philosophy.[16] Castoriadis differentiates between two interdependent and mutually constitutive levels of autonomy: the individual and collective. Individual autonomy emerges out of the project of collective autonomy. He conceptualizes individual autonomy with reference to the relation established between the conscious and the unconscious, stressing the possibility of individuals becoming conscious of unconscious contents, recognizing their origin and modifying them.

Thinking about individual autonomy and being in psychoanalytic terms, Castoriadis relies on Freud's proposed maxim, "Where Id was, Ego shall come to be." Castoriadis interprets this by saying:

> Ego must take place of Id—this can mean neither the suppression of drives, nor the elimination or the absorption of the unconscious. It is a matter of taking their place as an *agency of decision*. Autonomy would then be consciousness's rule over the unconscious (1987, p. 102).

In other words, autonomy "is the establishment of another relation between the discourse of the other and the subject's discourse," meaning not the rejection of other's influence, but a reflective attitude toward it (*ibid.*, p. 104). Autonomy aims at reflective and communicative negotiations between the subject and the other.

As previously seen, the whole socialization process of the individual has meant for him/her the internalization of social contents and ISS represented by the presence of the other. The acceptance of the other is initially necessary for the psyche to survive. As a direct consequence of the socialization and sublimation processes, the energetic life of the individual becomes regulated according to an organizing imaginary that has neither been created by, nor reflected on, nor even consciously appropriated by the individual. Desire and affect are heteronomously determined in the subject. Castoriadis writes:

> What is essential to heteronomy . . . on the level of the individual, is the domination of an autonomized imaginary which has assumed the function of defining for the subject both reality and desire. The "repression of drives" as such, the conflict between the "pleasure principle" and the "reality principle" do not constitute individual alienation. . . . The important conflict is that between drives and reality, on the one hand, and the imaginary development within the subject, on the other (1987, p. 103).

Individual autonomy is achieved by making clear the origin and the sense of the discourse of the other, and by affirming or negating its content in as much as it is the discourse of the other. Through reflectivity and deliberative activity, the subject can achieve a more autonomous stage in life. An autonomous individual is not defined as a person who has become pure Ego, but a person who questions what has been acquired by establishing a relation between the unconscious and the conscious, between lucidity and the function of the imaginary, in an attitude of the subject with respect to himself/herself. In this sense, individual autonomy means self-regulation, self-legislation, and opposition to heteronomy or the legislation or regulation by another. Castoriadis describes autonomy as the law created by the individual, as opposed to regulation by the unconscious, which is the law of one, but not of the individual. Castoriadis says "my discourse must take the place of the discourse of the other of a foreign discourse that is in me, ruling over me: speaking through myself" (*ibid.*, p. 102).[17]

However, individual autonomy does not suppose the total control of the conscious over the unconscious, nor does it mean the total elimination of the discourse of the other. These two would be impossible and unhistorical stages. For Castoriadis, individual autonomy also does not mean the rational mastery of inner nature or of the unconscious or the total repression of heteronomous desires. Furthermore, individual autonomy does not suppose a "total human being" or an "absolute subject" behind it; the unconsciously determining discourse of the other can never be fully appropriated.[18]

What autonomy does mean to Castoriadis is an endless process that does not terminate in a self-transparent individual or society. Autonomy is an attitude, an infinitely continuing project without a definable end state. Individual autonomy is not equal to Ego-control of given repressive practices of a socially given Ego-instance. It is neither restricted to a greater role for the individual radical imaginary.[19] It is more specifically characterized as an individual attitude that is instituted and backed by an ensemble of social imaginary signs.

Individual autonomy must contain conscious reflectiveness and the capacity for deliberate action. Castoriadis speaks of a type of consciousness that does not mean rational calculation or reckoning (these last two operations can be found in the unconscious as well). Instead, consciousness is where reflexivity is at work in self-questioning:

In reflectiveness we have something different: the possibility that the activity proper to the "subject" becomes an "object," the self being explicitly posited as a non-objective object or as an object that is an object simply by its being posited as such and not by nature (1989, p. 159).

Reflection implies the possibility of questioning oneself as representational activity. It presupposes and materializes the rupture of functionality.

Reflection is an attempt to break the closure in which individuals are necessarily immersed as a result of their personal and social history, and the history of the social-historical institution that has humanized the individuals. This attempt is always accompanied by the positing of new thinkable forms and figures created by the radical imagination. Reflective activity also makes psychoanalytical activity possible, but psychoanalysis is more than the reflection of the subject over itself and its own functioning conditions. It is also an opportunity for the analyzed individual to leave the parameters of his/her acquired psychical organization by opening his/her psyche to a new mode of being, a new history in which the subject is its co-author.[20]

Castoriadis' definition of individual autonomy necessarily encompasses political and social dimensions. The realization of autonomy cannot be conceived in its full scope except as a collective enterprise. Castoriadis states:

If autonomy is the relation in which others are always present as the otherness *and* as the self-ness of the subject, then autonomy can be conceived of, even in philosophical terms, only as a social problem and as a social relation (1987, p. 108).

Defined as an intersubjective relation, individual autonomy can be realized only as a moment of the social; it is the social which composes and also presupposes intersubjectivity. The social is not the sum of intersubjective networks (although it is that too), nor is it their simple product. Here it is worth remembering, because the social-historical is the anonymous collective whole, the impersonal-human element that fills every given social formation but also engulfs them. It is the union and the tension of the instituting and the instituted society, of history made and of history in the making.

Collective autonomy is the appropriation by the instituting power of the radical imaginary to create institutions and social imaginary significations, and to establish proper laws and practices. It presupposes questioning of social institution, and the creation of new significations, institutions, and political identities. It is the explicit recognition that social forms are self-generated without attribution to extrasocial sources. It is the recognition that society and history are social creations and that, as social collectives, societies are the product of such creations and of their own capacity of auto-institution (Castoriadis, 1991c, pp. 143–74). In relation to this, Castoriadis affirms:

Until when will humanity have the need to conceal the Abyss of the world and of itself behind instituted simulacra? The response, if response there be, can come only on the collective level and the individual level simultaneously. On both levels, it presupposes a radical alteration of one's relation to signification. I am autonomous only if I am the origin of what will be . . . and I know myself as such (1997h, p. 329).

Thus, as seen, there is always tension between instituted and instituting society, but society as a whole is usually unaware of it. If the awareness of the self-generation of society's limits and forms becomes instituted and rooted in its social imaginary, then a new relation between instituting and instituted society has appeared: this is the work of collective autonomy.

Collective autonomy produces individual autonomy and is at the same time grounded in it; they are two halves of the same whole. Neither can work alone. Individual autonomy lacks sense if it is detached from a collective political project. As Castoriadis noted, whoever wants to become free must be necessarily interested in the freedom of others, must be interested in the collective dimension of politics.

As discussed in the following chapter, the collective dimension of autonomy is linked by Castoriadis to the idea of politics and democracy. Politics and democracy as correlates of autonomy, are about auto-reflexivity and openness to institutions; that society does not halt before a conception given once and for all of what is just, equal, or free, but rather institutes itself in such a way that the questions of freedom, of justice, of equity and equality might always be posed a new within society. Democracy is the project of breaking the social closure at the collective level by appropriating the instituting power to institute societies that give their own rules.

The democratic project as Castoriadis conceives it comes straight out of his work with SouB. As seen in Chapter 1, at the end of 1960s Castoriadis faced an analytical challenge that demanded a comprehensive theory of society and history that contested determinism and left open room for a project of autonomy. The ontology of creation that he developed by integrating psychoanalysis into his work is the result of such questioning. This included not only his leaning-on explanation about the totality of the existing being and the way different regions or strata of the self related among themselves, but also an original way to define creation, imagination, social institutions, and autonomy. This chapter has presented the conceptual basis upon which Castoriadis' philosophical and political contributions stand, which were initially elaborated in *The Imaginary Institution of Society*. It is in this work that Castoriadis presents his new understandings of subjectivity—mainly inspired by Freudian psychoanalysis—and agency, giving imagination an ontological weight. The way he defines the subject, the existing relationships between psyche and society, and the instituted and instituting society becomes pivotal for envisioning a new way to conceive history, social change, and creation.

Chapter 3

Agency and Autonomy in Castoriadis

In the previous chapter, I presented the main concepts of Castoriadis' ontology of creation, explaining his own particular developments such as the radical imaginary, the instituted and instituting imaginaries, and the social-historical. This chapter focuses on Castoriadis' innovative notions of the subject: "agency, the production of social meaning, and social change". It will also discuss the weaknesses and potentialities of these concepts by reviewing critiques made by other intellectual figures from the fields of philosophy and social and political theory. As a corollary of these debates, the notion of autonomy will be examined, presenting some of the inherent tensions of this concept.

Agency and the Subject

As seen in Chapter 2, the concept of the subject is a pivotal one for Castoriadis as he seeks to overcome ontological dualisms without falling into realist or rationalist interpretations. The subject plays a central role, invested with creative and representational faculties through which meaning and social institutions come to existence. Though Castoriadis centers the subject in the philosophical, anthropological, and political terrains, his conceptual elaboration of the subject is a post-metaphysical attempt that contests any form of transcendentalism. As discussed, Castoriadis approaches the subject as a social product whose subjective formation is the result of the sublimation process and the internalization of the imaginary social significations (ISS) by the psyche.

Moreover, Castoriadis rejects any essentialist or teleological vision of the subject and its historical dimension. Embedded in the imaginary of society, the subject's historical development does not suppose a natural or progressive movement toward the realization of its essence. In Castoriadis' conception nothing refers to positivist or objectivist versions in the history of anthropological or philosophical thought. He rejects the idea of a pure, abstract, disembodied rational agent as well as structures that would determine the subject's psychical representations, social practices, or institutions.

Drawing on Freud's work on the unconscious, Castoriadis formulates a theory of the subject that contests the linguistic-turn tendency while simultaneously building an innovative theory of representation. He takes into account the conscious and the unconscious and derives significant consequences for an understanding, not only of the process of subjective formation in the individual, but also a new mode of being of the psyche and the social. However Castoriadis understands the physical and biological dimensions of the subject differently than Freud. His formulation of the totality of the existing being characterized by the undetermined relationships among its different strata allows him to dissociate from the positivistic aspects of Freud's work and present a new way of conceiving the human psyche as radical imagination, an undetermined and creative imagination.

As a central idea in the subject's definition, the radical imagination constitutes a particular characteristic of the human being—however, radical imagination is not understood as an ultimate foundation of the subject. As Kalyvas clarifies:

> The psyche does not contain an absolute meaning that is gradually externalized and realized in the form of the subject; it does not consist of an a priori that is both logical and ontological, atemporal and universal, always the same, penetrating every human creation. The radical imagination is not something located beneath or behind the subject as a separate and independent entity. . . . [Castoriadis does not] argue that beneath the various stages of socialization there is something authentic whose sealed mouth needs only to be opened. . . . The psyche is a psychoanalytical category with ontological implications, not a metaphysical-transcendental one (1998a, p. 181).

As radical imagination has been extensively defined and discussed in Chapter 2, it is apposite to discuss precisely what it is not, in the light of possible questions that can be raised.

Castoriadis never poses the radical imagination as a primordial essence, nor as something waiting to be "finally discovered" in the subject. The radical imagination does not presuppose any type of development that would mark a new epoch in the life of the spirit in the Hegelian sense, even less so in the phylogenetical development in the Freudian sense. Nor is there a preestablished telos for the subject or for society, or a single conception of what it would mean for the subject to have a good life. The radical imagination is a condition for the subject to represent its reality and create institutions; it is also a precondition for the subject to become conscious of already being a representation, a social creation that can be put into question and that can transform him or herself and their institutions. The radical imagination does not exist alone as an essentiality without society. The fact that the radical imagination makes it possible for the psyche to generate meaning does not mean that the psyche alone can generate institutions. Castoriadis constantly reminds readers that the psyche generates phantasies, but not social institutions. That is why he emphasizes the irreducibility of the social imaginary and the radical imaginary in his leaning-on theory.

The leaning-on nature of the strata of living-being demonstrates how the subject should be understood as a social-historical creation, the result of a sustained conflict between the instituting imaginary and the instituted imaginary—as defined in Chapter 2—that creates and sanctions the ISS and the social institutions in which the individual is socialized. As a social-historical creation, the subject is the product of radical and social imaginaries that does not have a preordained fate. The fact that in Castoriadis' theory the psyche is not naturally predestined to be socialized, and is never completely socialized, does not mean that it isn't a necessary pole for the social-historical creation, or that it cannot become social. Nor does it mean that Castoriadis was unable to explain the mediation between the individual and the social as Habermas has stated.

Habermas found it illogical to explain the process of socialization as beginning with an a social individual. Instead, Habermas postulated the contrary. He explained socialization as a harmonic process where humans transform from an original state as a prelinguistic living-being into social individuals who integrate into their community, owing to their linguistic capacity:

> The individuation of the neonate, which within the womb of the mother has been an exemplar of the species as a pre-linguistic living being, and thus could be explained biologically in terms of a combination of a finite number of elements quite adequately, once born can only be conceived as a process of socialization. To be sure, here socialization cannot be conceived as the adaptation to society of an already given individuality, but as that which itself produces an individuated being (Habermas, 1996, pp. 127–8).

Immersed as he is in the linguistic turn, Habermas does not see an original individuality or an original self-consciousness in the human being. Instead, he posits intersubjective processes where relations are symbolically mediated. He accepts the premise that the individuation of the subject is a linguistically mediated process of socialization and the simultaneous constitution of a life history that is conscious itself. Unlike Castoriadis, Habermas does not take into account the unconscious dimension in this process. For him the original human specificity is restricted to a proto-linguistic condition that naturally enables the subject to enter the socialization process in order to become an individuated being (Habermas, 1992, p. 151).

As a consequence of this premise, another theoretical difference between Habermas and Castoriadis emerges. Habermas (1987) questioned Castoriadis' mediation between the individual and society by stating:

Castoriadis cannot provide us with a figure for the mediation between the individual and society. Society breaks down the childlike monads and transforms them. The type proper to the socially institutionalized world is impressed upon the individual. Thus the process of socialization is depicted on the model of crafts production. The socialized individual is produced and, as in Durkheim, remains divided into a monad and a member of society. [In Castoriadis] Intrapsychic conflicts are not internally linked with social ones; instead, psyche and society stand in a kind of metaphysical opposition to one another (p. 334).

As with Whitebook's critique of the monadic stage, the Habermasian position also omits the anaclisis or leaning-on explanation that elucidates the relationship between the psychical and the social poles of the individual. Rather than observing the way Castoriadis theorizes the relation between the strata of the existing-being in the context of his ontology of creation, Whitebook and Habermas look at the relationship between specific strata (mediations for them) in isolation, disregarding the very notion of creation, or at best, giving this central issue insufficient attention.

However, an enormous distinction separates their critiques. Unlike Whitebook, Habermas rejects an account of the inner nature of the subject distinct from its linguistic nature, a substantive fact that involves other theoretical consequences. Contrary to Castoriadis, Habermas—who does not accept the Freudian notion of the unconscious as a way to explain the inner extralinguistic reality of the subject—considers the subject as a biological living being exemplar until it smoothly enters the process of socialization at birth. For him, the original human specificity is restricted to a proto-linguistic condition. He limits his elaborations about the extralinguistic inner reality of the subject to the linguistification of the unconscious.

As Dews (1995, p. 179) points out, some questions emerge from this Habermasian position, where there is no prelinguistic awareness of the self. Emphasizing this point of Habermas, Dews writes:

> With regard to the tension between conscious and unconscious, Habermas' thought is directed towards reflecting upon and eliminating the unconscious social processes which hamper the rationality of communication, while being aware that this can never be definitively achieved. Finally, the question of the genesis of linguistic intersubjectivity itself, and in general of the historical transition from nature to culture, is no less of a problem for Habermas. . . . There remains the question of . . . whether the final achievements of communicative rationality would simply be the fulfillment of a tendency present in nature from the very beginning, or whether a certain opacity of natural compulsion will always remain opposed to, and capable of thwarting, the struggle for rational transparency (p. 186).

Habermas, without resolving the question of the external and internal extralinguistic realities of the subject, presents a determined transition from nature to culture in the human subject. The Habermasian framework cannot accept an entity with a nonlinguistic dimension that is not predestined to be a social being as an original subject.

On the contrary, Castoriadis posits the existence of an original undetermined subject possessing an unconscious and nonlinguistic dimension. He distinguishes clearly between the nonlinguistic, the prelinguistic, and the linguistic dimensions of the individual as he explains the creative imagination in a holistic relationship between the psyche and the society. Far from being a metaphysical opposition, the relationship between the psychic and social poles of the individual was explained by Castoriadis as a polarity where the psyche and society are never in total contradiction or opposition. The opposites are conceived simultaneously, and one element refers to the other in a movement of creation. As highlighted in the previous chapter, psyche and society together create a new ontological level. The new creations, the new emergences, are not necessary consequences of previous strata but are new strata of the total-being, radically different from "the previous ones"; this is how the relationship between the psychic and the social has to be understood.

Habermas disagrees with this point and further states that in Castoriadis' formulation of political autonomy he "replaces" the self-instituting subject with the self-instituting society, in which autonomous action as intramundane praxis is assimilated to the language-creating, world-projecting, world-devouring praxis of the social demiurge itself. As a consequence, Habermas argues, it fits the personification of society as a demiurge that releases ever-new world-types from itself (Habermas, 1987, p. 332–3).[1] Once again Habermas disregards the relation Castoriadis establishes between the psyche and society misunderstanding—as Kalyvas (1998b, p. 17) notes—the instituting dimension of autonomy and how it supposes neither a homogenous social subject nor the traditional notion of popular sovereignty.[2]

Society is a new ontological level that makes possible the existence of the human being, which has to go through a painful socialization process that is never completed. It is this ever present deficit of socialization of the psyche that prevents the permanent closure of the living being and enables the creation of social institutions and imaginary social significations. For this reason, Castoriadis claims that in humans there is not an inherent disposition to socialization; accepting that the contrary would cancel out the notion of radical imagination and its emancipation potentiality and creative agency.

The creative psychical capacity and its transgressive power are indeed central qualities of Castoriadis' subject. This explains his rejection of the subject as merely the inscription of cultural codes, structures of language, or power relationships, which was the view sustained by poststructuralist theorists. Castoriadis refuses to consider the subject as an entity entirely infused by externally imposed social practices and institutions. He controverts such interpretations, because they lead to the disappearance of the subject's agency and autonomy and produced social conformity and homogeneity (Castoriadis, 1997t, pp. 32–43).

Agency, for Castoriadis, refers to the relationship between the individual and society, and to the individual's self-constitution within their specific social context in order to become subjects of action capable of transforming their reality in a manner free of total determination. Castoriadis opts for rethinking a self-reflexive agent capable of conceiving and transforming the very world that had provided it with its identity. He sees the subject and its subjectivity as problems that require fine theorization, because without it, every notion of ethical responsibility vanishes and the subject is reduced to a fiction, living in a world where individuals are enslaved and oppressed by society. A theory of subjectivity is needed for Castoriadis in order to explain any self-reflective capacity that would allow the subject to get distanced from his/her subjective contents, as well as from society, in order to transform them. He aims at building a theory of subjectivity and agency that enables autonomous possibilities for the subject and his/her society.

Interestingly, Castoriadis' understanding of subjectivity implies both a social construct, invisibly governed by social imaginary significations, and a self-reflective and transgressive potential capable of consciously modifying social imaginary contents. Subjectivity is a concrete form of psychical organization shaped by instituted imaginary significations. However, it resists full penetration by social content. Given his need to keep a distance between the subject and society in order to make room for a privatistic dimension and for creative agency in the subject, Castoriadis rejects the idea of fully integrated and socialized subjectivities. He theorizes a possible introspection for the subject to analyze his/her own subjective configuration. This introspection would enable a self-reflective distance in which to see him or herself as "another." The subject becomes conscious that self-realization is not a natural deployment of his or her own essence, but is self-forming and value-positing within a relative, historical, and cultural formation.

In this sense, the constructivist position taken by Castoriadis toward the subject is not exhausted in recognizing the individual only as a bearer of society. On the contrary, his theoretical explanation aims precisely at equipping the subject with means of resistance and creation, creation of a new and undetermined eidos.

In sum, Castoriadis elaborates a theory of the subject that takes psychical stratification and subjective formation into consideration providing an account for the social imposition on the individual psyche. Likewise, his theory of the subject carefully keeps individual and social space for auto-reflection as a road to agency and autonomy. The psychical stratification of the subject demonstrates how the subject is immersed and grounded in the social world, while at the same time the subject is able to stand apart from the social realm and become a new creation. The subject is not reduced to a passive product of superior forces that operate behind its back. Through the concept of autonomy, Castoriadis reclaims critical self-reflectiveness and the subject's agency and capacity to give itself its own laws and institutions.

The Creation of Social Meaning and Representation: Imaginary Social Significations and Social Institutions

Castoriadis' elaborations on the creation of social meaning and institutions challenge functionalist, unilineal, and evolutionist theories of culture and history. They contest ideas such as the "end of history," narratives of social reconciliation, and illusions of a complete re-appropriation of social institutions from an alienated state to one of conscious control.

Social meaning is closely tied to Castoriadis' theoretical elaboration about representation and his concepts of ISS and social institutions. It derives from the representational activities deployed by the individual radical imaginary and by the social imaginary. The radical imagination, as the faculty enabling the activity of constructing significations and providing sense to the world, constitutes the concept to which the emergence of meaning and institutions is referred.[3] ISS and social institutions instantiate society. They are already present in the individuals and the society composing and legitimizing it; in other words, they are a required condition for the subject and his or her society to come into existence.

Social institutions and meanings are creations that are not absolute, static, or unchangeable, nor do they have a single and definite end that determines once and for all the social individuals that have been fabricated under their grids. Those are seen simultaneously as necessarily imposed on the subject and, at the same time, as something from which socialized individuals can abstract and voluntarily transform themselves. This means that social meaning and institutions that the subject has to accept are givens in society within which the subject has to become functional. However, they also constitute an optional and discretionary choice for both the individual subject and the social collective.

In this understanding of social meaning and institutions, society has ontological weight, yet is not invested with supreme powers that overrun the subject entirely. Castoriadis' alternative prevents meaning and institutions from being understood only as products of society where the subject is a blind operator, whose intervention and capacity to create and recreate its own social institutions and practices is limited, or whose ability to transform them lacks sense because it cannot bring any innovations or substantially different social forms into being.

By considering social meaning to be a creation that emerges from the social-historical where its two poles, the psyche and society, are at work—Castoriadis involves subject and society equally in the process of generating and institutionalizing SIS and meaning, without conceiving them as determined or fixed. Meaning becomes, in this framework, a magmatic organization that involves different dimensions—strata—the relation of which is never given in a mathematical or determined way, and where none of the strata rules over the others.

The magmatic organization of social meaning expresses itself in society through social imaginary significations that result from the flow of representations, affects, and intentions (the individual imaginary of the psyche) and the open stream of the anonymous collective (the social imaginary). These significations are entities around which the meaning-world of society is structured. They are the organizing principles behind the representation of the world of objects and relations and provide the kernel around which society creates its reality and its institutions. They are intertwined units of representations, affects, and intentions that cannot be simplified into something like the signified in a sign system. These significations can be, but are not necessarily, given to the consciousness of individual subjects in society; they are neither noemata nor noesis[4] (Castoriadis, 1987, pp. 359, 364).

In other words, meaning can be understood as embedded in the totality of social institutions. Social meaning is everything that supersedes, overcomes the identitary dimension (functional-instrumental) and that which individuals from that society consider as a value, that which becomes instituted in the social world through the operations of legein and teukhein (Castoriadis, 2000b, p. 202).

The operations of legein and teukhein "articulate" the ambiguous magma of imaginary significations and institute order. They provide the necessary stability for social meaning to be materialized and to survive for the instituted society. These operations are used by societies and their individuals to organize, structure, and control their world. They act upon the intrinsic ambiguity and contingency present in relations among different strata, such as the relationship between the biological and the social world, or in the relationship between the flow of representations and affects. Socially instituted signification systems—language, meaning (legein)—and socially instituted systems of practice (teukhein) are built on ambiguous ground that allows for alternative definitions of elements and sets (Castoriadis, 1987, pp. 360–1). These explicit organizational steps take up the evanescent and indeterminate self-organization of the magmatically given and expand on it. Instituted ensembles of imaginary significations behind the explicit operations of legein and teukhein reduce complexity and introduce contingent constructions.

However, while the stability of meaning and of instituted society is a constitutive condition of possibility for the human world, instituting society constantly works toward change and innovation. The work of instituting society always begins in a historical situation from the basis of instituted society, but its innovations constitute irreducible, nondetermined acts of positing and creation (*ibid.*, p. 369). In this sense, the social-historical is explained as ordered, settled, enduring, and stable through the operations of legein and teukhein, but at the same time as creative potentiality: the source of change and the possibility of new social forms.

This framework where the instituting/instituted world, rather than a confrontation of contingency and ambiguity versus stability and certainty in the creation process, presents these two pairs without posing them as mutually exclusive. Social meaning and representation are simultaneously continuous and discontinuous, contingent and certain, ambiguous and unambiguous. Although they are instituted and sanctioned by societies for the purposes of signification and interpretation, they are anything but fixed, territorialized, or stable. They are mobile and fluid, yet solid enough to socialize and create individuals who can be functional within certain social orders and reproduce their constitutive social imaginary significations.

Heteronomy, Autonomy, and Social Change

Castoriadis considers the dynamics of social change as inherent in society. Though society is not always aware of it, it is constantly in a tension between permanency and change, between the instituted and instituting. Social institutions and ISS survive thanks to their own closure, however, they also contain a drive for change. Despite the fact that ISS have a static character, which responds to their self-reproduction and closure tendencies, they are also constantly threatened by the instituting power as a source of irritation, adaptation, and innovation (*ibid.*, p. 371).

On the one hand, society aims to maintain itself as naturally ordered and permanent. Social change is always countered by defenses that are held in by every society against threatening or contradicting central significations. These defenses are expressed in its heteronomous state.[5] Individuals are always prepared to respond according to the ruling imaginary, what Castoriadis calls the radical ground power of society: a power that is implicit, impersonal, and non-locatable.

Nevertheless, on the other hand, societies are always on the edge of internally collapsing and producing changes in their principal institutions. The defenses used by individuals and institutions to maintain themselves fail because of the ongoing threats in multiple directions made by the instituting society (Castoriadis, 1991c, p. 150). The radical imaginary provides the conditions for constantly transgressing the semantic and social closure of instituted society. The innovating activity of instituting society never ends, and the closure of a given instituted world is always incomplete, due to the magmatic character of its constitutive ontological basis. In this sense, change is intrinsic to the social-historical and the total closure of a society is impossible and ahistorical.

Autonomy

The key to social change and emancipation for Castoriadis is autonomy. Individual and collective autonomy arise from the dynamic exercised between instituted and instituting society. Autonomy is the ultimate goal of social change, as Castoriadis sees it, a value in itself that can be contrasted to closure and the heteronomous states of societies.

Furthermore, understood in terms of autonomy, social change is plausible in a heteronomous society whose members can become aware of the social nature of their laws and, through social change, become conscious authors of their own mandates and institutions. Castoriadis believes that social change can bring about emancipatory social orders. To break the closure of society is to change a given heteronomous relationship between society and the social imaginary. In other words, any attempt at social change, including theory, should begin with the premise that alienation *appears* in the relationship between society and the social imaginary, but is *not* this relationship.

Castoriadis gives individual change and autonomy psychoanalytical emphasis. He appeals to psychoanalytic theory to explain an instance of self-reflectivity that permits the individual to establish a different relationship between the unconscious and conscious. Acknowledging the fact that the individual's consciousness could never exhaust its unconscious contents, Castoriadis defends the psychoanalytical principle that the individual can become conscious of the origin and psychical function of their wills, desires, and motivations, and in so doing, become more autonomous before them. This is to say that the individual has more elements of judgment, and can more properly decide his or her actions, when knowing the unconscious motivations that lay behind them.

In reference to social collectives, Castoriadis postulates social change as a product of social struggles over institutions in an attempt to appropriate a greater amount of instituting power, gain more public deliberation, and alter instituted norms and values by positing new ones according to the common ends that the community posits for itself. However, it is important to remember that Castoriadis never postulates a naturally given collective subject or even the idea of popular dominion. The instituting power cannot be located in one instance of the social or incarnated by a transcendental subjectivity. It is anonymous, realized through the pursuit of an undetermined number of particular ends, and escapes all efforts to circumscribe it.

While Castoriadis differentiates between the individual and social forms of autonomy, both of them simultaneously require a collective project of autonomy, as well as auto-reflective and autonomous individual identities. Neither can be thought of independently: they are mutually dependent. As Kalyvas notes (1998 b, p. 18), Castoriadis alludes to a conflictual model of politics where a new social eidos does not emerge from single individual acts, decisions, or instaurations of procedures. They are seen as an unintended effect of political and social struggles, as the by-products of antagonistic interactions that under certain conditions can coalesce into a deliberate and lucid project, as in the case of the project of autonomy and democracy (Castoriadis, 1991a, p. 222).

Legitimacy and normative status of autonomy

The concept of autonomy in Castoriadis has a normative character, though, as Kalyvas states (1998a, pp. 172, 179), it cannot be reduced to a critical norm restricted for use as a principle for testing the validity of rules, laws, and institutions of existing democracies. Autonomy is a political project. This normative character has, however, opened further discussion in relation to Castoriadis' theory. The intention to introduce a normative standard without falling into metaphysical or foundational lines of thinking has been interpreted as containing unresolved tensions, as Habermas (1987), Honneth (1986), and Poltier (1989) have noted.[6]

The concept of autonomy and its status as a critical, impartial, and normative criterion has been questioned on the basis of Castoriadis' approach to the problem of validity. Considering Castoriadis' arguments on validity, it could be said that he was not able to overcome relativism because it is not possible to derive a normative political program or standard from his theory. This critique is based on the fact that for Castoriadis, "meaning and validity are social-historical creations. They constitute the mode of being of the institution . . . .They are expressive of the fundamental fact that each society is a being-for-itself and that it creates a world of its own" (1997c, p. 387).

Ultimately, the issue upon which this critique is built is none other than the lack of a foundation to equip Castoriadis' concept of autonomy to operate as a critical normative standard. As Kalyvas (1998a, p. 164) notes, other questions could be raised along this line of argumentation:

If there can be no appeal to something higher than effectively actual individuals, nor any objective extra-social standpoint, nor any prior transcendental moral order, given our partial interests and subjective preferences, why and how can autonomy claim the positional status of a critical norm?

Castoriadis puts it this way:

> What can be the measure if no extra-social standard exists, what could and should be the law if no external norm could serve for it as a term of comparison, what can be life over the Abyss once it is understood that it is absurd to assign to the Abyss a precise figure, be it that of an idea, a value, or a meaning determined once and for all (Kalyvas, 1998a, p. 179, quoting Castoriadis (1997h, p. 329).

Castoriadis does recognize the fact that there is no absolute justification for autonomy, and that its legitimation can only be found in the social collective. It is only the social collective that can legitimate it.[7] However, to infer that his theory falls into relativism because he did not provide extrasocial standards, external norms, or precise figures, ideas, values, or meanings determined once and for all that could serve as a term of comparison is to misunderstand his conception of autonomy. As discussed in previous sections, Castoriadis aims to avoid any form of relativism by proposing a postmetaphysical form of autonomy that does not contain or consult absolute and/or ultimate foundations. He shows, through his concept of autonomy, how it is possible to conceive a normative standard that enables us to choose and judge between social institutions, without presupposing specific contents already inferred or known, rooted in transcendental or ultimate principles. He justifies a conception of the norm of validity that simultaneously presents a defined critical criterion of superior validity and acknowledges its inherent relationship and consubstantiality with the social-historical character of meaning.[8] In other words, Castoriadis justifies the superiority of autonomy as a norm of validity by presenting a new understanding of it, and providing a new way in which it should be addressed in the realm of politics.[9]

Castoriadis is aware that relativism is an easy position to fall into, once it is accepted that there is no foundational or transcendental principles that can substantiate a source of validity (1997c, pp. 388–9). Against a relativist position that proclaimed that difference is indifferent, he emphasizes the distinction between de facto or positive validity, which is the validity of each society's institutions for itself, and the de jure validity, which allows questioning of society's parameters. He writes:

We raise the question of the *de jure* validity of this rule [of de facto or positive validity]. We ask ourselves: what *ought we* to think of this rule and *what ought we to make of it?* We acknowledge the infinite variety of historical *nomoi*, and we pose the question: Do all these *nomoi* have the same *value*, and what *nomos* ought we to want for ourselves? That is equivalent to saying that we introduce (we accept) the meta category of the *de jure validity*. It is easy to show that it is equivalent to the *instauration* of reflection and *deliberation*, both taken in the radical sense (1997c, pp. 388–9).

As seen, Castoriadis justifies with the capacity of auto-reflection and deliberation what he theorizes as the innate disposition of every human being to re-imagine what another human being has already imagined (*ibid.*, p. 390). But to avoid misunderstanding, it has to be said that Castoriadis does not transform this creative potential of the psyche, upon which autonomy is grounded, into an ultimate foundation. Instead, the products of the psyche—its creations—are to be examined under the criterion of autonomy. The psyche does not contain an absolute meaning that ought to be gradually realized in the form of the subject; it is not an a priori. The radical imagination is not something located beneath or behind the subject as a separate or independent entity.

Castoriadis complements his substantiation of the normative content of the concept of autonomy with the collective dimension of autonomy: the political autonomy, which he links to a new conception of politics and democracy. These are characterized by auto-reflexivity and openness to institutions. Society does not freeze before a conception, given once and for all, of what is just, equal, or free, but rather institutes itself in such a way that the questions of freedom, of justice, and of equity and equality might always be posed a new within the framework of the "normal" functioning of society.

This original understanding of democracy articulates the instituting/instituted power of the radical imaginary. Democracy is the form that makes possible political autonomy where the instituting power of society operates, creating and instituting new social institutions in a conscious, reflective, and deliberative way. Castoriadis does not understand democracy as a set of procedures, nor collective autonomy as merely the simple sovereign manifestation of majorities. He conceives democracy as the real possibility of a collective subjectivity that questions and adapts its institutions through the effective participation of its citizens. It is the capacity to reflect as a collective about itself and interrogate its laws and create new ones. In this sense, Castoriadis again provides a justification of collective rights (one that would encompass procedures and mechanisms) that guarantees the debate of arguments and reasons in conditions of free speech, free thinking, and free examination.

Putting aside the discussion of democracy for a moment, it is possible to say that for Castoriadis the concept of autonomy —both individual and collective—as a corollary can be seen as a norm of validity defined as a condition and not as a foundation. Castoriadis made it clear:

To the question "Why autonomy? Why reflection?" there is no foundational answer, no response "upstream." There is a social-historical *condition*: the project of autonomy, reflection, deliberation, and reason have already been created, they are already there, and they belong to our tradition. But this *condition* is not a *foundation* (1997c, p. 394).

It is apposite to remember that autonomy is for Castoriadis a social-historical creation that contains critical potentiality and makes room for overcoming heteronomy in society. Nevertheless, its condition of creation does not necessarily legitimize it. For Castoriadis, creation as such does not necessarily have an essentially positive connotation. Castoriadis reminds us that *Macbeth* was a social creation in the same way that Auschwitz was. Social creations do not have an intrinsic foundation or legitimacy. He is rightly aware that social creations gain legitimacy only to the extent that their authors—or participants in a social institution—provide it. For Castoriadis, the project of autonomy is an end and a guide, but does not involve determined solutions. It does not effectively resolve actual situations (*ibid.*, p. 400). The aim of autonomy to break closure does not suppose in itself a specific and determined social form. Autonomy is a creation and, as such, it is not an event but a continuous creative and dynamic process. This is why autonomy cannot be equated to specific historical contents or absolute forms. As Klooger (2009, p. 320) correctly states, autonomy cannot be identified solely with a specific individual psyche, or society. Autonomy must be understood as distributed among the psychical and collective poles to varying degrees, in various senses, and at various moments. Autonomy is neither a necessary historical consequence of preexisting cultural settings nor the self-reflective forms that produced this singular creation in the ancient Greek polis.

Authors inscribed in a post-transcendental phenomenological perspective have questioned this conception of autonomy as a radical creation or alterity and an unprecedented form of self-reflection with no previous existence in any other historical and cultural contexts except the ancient Greek polis, for example, Arnason[10] (1989, 1994, 2001, 2003, 2011), who elaborates on the work of Eisenstadt (1986, 2001, 2003) and the civilizations of axial age approach (2003, pp. 227–8).[11] Drawing on the hermeneutical tradition and the role played by interpretation, he questions Castoriadis' understanding of that tradition. Arnason appreciates the importance of Castoriadis' notion of the imaginary as the creative element present in cultural formations, which contributes to the analysis of patterns of meaning at a civilizational level. However, he states that the concept of imagination needs to be interpreted in the light of a hermeneutical transformation, relating it to the constitution of meaning and patterns of world interpretation (1994, pp. 155–70). Understanding the articulation of cultural formations as an intercultural horizon of varying trans-subjective and trans-objective contexts of meaning, Arnason states that the civilizational axial age must be interpreted within the indeterminate, ambiguous, and enigmatic character of the world (p. 232). In this context, Arnason believes Castoriadis fails to acknowledge the phenomenological interpretation of the world as a shared horizon, where the hermeneutical dimension of creativity—or better put, the interpretive element of creation—is not acknowledged in his ontology (2003, p. 228; 2011, p. 115).

As Adams (2005; 2007, p. 55) explains, the crucial difference between Castoriadis and Arnason rests in their approaches to interpretation and its link to the world *tout court*. Castoriadis repudiates the hermeneutical aspect of world interpretation whereas Arnason sees it as crucial. Consequently, this difference also reflects their diverging understandings of autonomy and the social-historical as creation. Arnason (1989, p. 26) emphasizes the culturological aspects of social-historical creativity, meaning by this that the cultural component of social institutions should be understood from a hermeneutical perspective rather than from an ontological one (Arnason quoted by Adams, 2007, p. 55). Arnason states that creation is interpretive and contextual, and disputes the concept of creation in Castoriadis. For Arnason, creation *ex nihilo* must presuppose "something" that is—however creatively—interpreted and transformed.

Adams shares this vision with Arnason and, rather than validating the idea of ex-nihilum creation, she also prefers to talk about "contextual creation" where a hermeneutic qualification is needed.[12] She argues that Castoriadis rejects the following three levels of interpretive activity inherent to creation (2005, p. 35):[13] First, interpretation includes a creative moment; second, undetermined SIS always requires interpretation and elaboration; and third, the social-historical world occurs in the context of interpretation and transformation of already existing historical constellations of meaning.

This observation is anchored by Adams's critical position before Castoridian notions of creation and "leaning-on", a position shared by Arnason and other critics previously discussed, including Habermas and

Whitebook. Despite their distinct theoretical takes, their common critique refers to the relationships among strata and to the idea of alterity and creation as a radical other, as an unprecedented form that does not respond to, nor is a consequence of, previous social forms or latent meanings that could be interpreted.

These critiques boil down to the challenging Castoridian idea of origin that is presupposed in the circle of creation and is the consequence of his attempt to break with determinacy. In order to appreciate Castoriadis' position, one must not get trapped in the chicken and egg question, but—as Klooger (2009, p. 95) puts it—acknowledge the ultimate seriousness of this riddle while dodging its apparent insolubility. I agree with the explanation Ciaramelli (1997) has provided in relation to origin. Following Castoriadis, he states:

Thinking of the origin in a radical way amounts to thinking of the movement by which what does not proceed from something else—what does not have its origin elsewhere—comes to itself, has within itself precisely the ontological energy to detach itself from itself and to exist as origin. In its primordial sense, then, origin is *self-origin*: it is, becomes, and is known starting from itself. This self-presupposition of the origin constitutes the very advent of Being, its unmotivated and permanent upsurge, which has to be thought in terms of creation. Human creation responds to this ontological genesis, to its indeterminacy and its incompletion—and, consequently, to its temporality. At once individual and collective—that is, both psychical and social—human creation alone can give meaning to ontological genesis (p. 45).

In Ciaramelli's view (1997, p. 64), Castoriadis' ontology of creation, which embeds its own self-presupposition and origin, constitutes his major contribution and reopens questions that modern rationalization has denied. However, this unique way of thinking of the Being necessarily poses aporias inherent to the indeterminacy and the Chaos, the Abyss, and the Groundlessness from which humanity emerges (1997h, p. 311). In consequence, creation and the articulation of the world are not about harmonious, smooth, and continuous processes—even though they do involve continuity to a certain extent.

Nevertheless, this explanation does not satisfy Arnason and Adams who, inspired by Habermas, are interested in a theory about the articulation of the world that draws on mediation and mutual understanding, rather than on an unbridgeable chasm of radical alterity.[14]

I will avoid the already discussed arguments and responses Castoriadis presents before this critique. However, Adams and Arnason introduce new elements that are worth discussing, such as meaning and interpretation, and the existing relation between intercultural contexts, history, continuity, and discontinuity. Smith (2010) also echoes their interest in Castoriadis' developments. As Arnason and Adams do, Smith wants to read Castoriadis as a post-Heideggerian hermeneuticist whose ontology does not do justice to interpretation, especially, in relation to the notion of creation (2010, p. 5).[15]

I disagree with these scholars who attempt to place Castoriadis within the hermeneutical and phenomenological traditions and their later developments. Furthermore, I do not agree with Arnason and Adams, the latter of whom states that Castoriadis: 1) is reluctant to explore the imaginary dimension of contexts of meaning as distinct from the ensidic (Adams, 2007, p. 55) and, 2) "misses that each society institutes the world in a concrete, positive sense that is imposed on a broader horizon" (*ibid.*, p. 58) because he rejects the creative aspects of interpretation. My view is the contrary, that is, Castoriadis theorizes the creative faculty and the imaginary dimension of meaning, taking into account the ensidic logic of the world without denying the central role of interpretation.

To be sure, in Castoriadis' theory each society interprets and elaborates on its SIS, its existing meaning, and its social institutions. "Each and every society creates, within its cognitive closure or its closure of meaning, its own world" (Castoriadis, 1991f, p. 37). Moreover, Castoriadis accepts that creations emerge within already existing historical contexts of meaning that leave room for interpretation and transformation. However, interpretation does not refer to immanent or latent elements, forms, or relationships throughout history or within cultures. This is the main break Castoriadis attempts to make in relation to inherited ontology. Creation is not production, not the bringing forth of an exemplar of a preexisting eidos.

The social-historical is not reducible to ordained intelligible elements. It is not constituted by elements that have been combined in a specific form and that can be recombined in another (*ibid.*, p. 35). As the social-historical domain is defined as creation, so is history. History is the self-deployment and self-alteration of society, an alteration whose very forms are each time the creation of the society considered. Castoriadis posits history as creation and destruction of forms, or eide (*ibid.*, p. 34). Nonetheless, the social-historical as creation ex-nihilum does not mean creation in a worldless vacuum, it is not literally given out of nothing. Society leans upon the first natural stratum in order to erect an edifice of significations invested with meaning upon which new creations can emerge (*ibid.*, p. 41).[16]

In sum, ex-nihilum creations are conditioned and limited by the ensidic dimension and the existing instituted world, without being determined by them. It is only in this sense that Castoriadis accepts that there is interpretation or even transformation of the instituted world. However, neither interpretation nor transformation involves immanent forms, elements, or latent contexts of meaning.

Unlike Arnason, Castoriadis is not interested in theorizing trans-cultural elements present in society that guarantee history a certain continuity. Despite the fact that for Castoriadis society tends to heteronomy and closure, his theory also provides conceptual instruments with which to understand moments of rupture, social change, discontinuity, and creation. The fact that society and history are simultaneously continuous and discontinuous is precisely shown in what he is pointing out with the idea of creation and is implicit in other concepts such as SIS and social institutions. While acknowledging the necessary continuity for new creations to occur through the instituted imaginary, the discontinuity brought about through the instituting imaginary makes new creations possible.

These different perspectives are also reflected in the way Castoriadis and Arnason understand autonomy. While Castoriadis sees the emergence of autonomy as a creation, rupture, discontinuity, and openness in society, Arnason sees it as part of a continuum within the axial of civilizations. For the latter, the polis is the result of a long-term process characterized by formative shifts, divergences, and turning points where the project of autonomy in the polis qua polis was developed through a long process between the eighth and the fifth centuries B.C.E.

In other words, Arnason (2001, p. 175) and Adams (2005, pp. 25–41) understand autonomy as a contextual creation where intracultural aspects in the plurality of ancient Greek poleis are at stake. By sustaining that self-reflective practices and the explicit questioning of one's own social institutions preceded the invention of autonomy in the ancient Greek polis, they discuss Castoriadis' position by which the creation of autonomy is linked to the invention of philosophy and democracy being born at the same time and place in the ancient Greek polis.

Arnason studies a variety of self-reflective practices throughout history, where autonomy and heteronomy should be seen as variously intertwined and mutually relativizing aspects of historical patterns (2001, p. 203). In his view, Castoriadis polarizes autonomy and heteronomy as binary opposites and thereby consigns world history to a heteronomous state.

Smith (2010, pp. 159–89) backs Arnason's position, arguing that although autonomy can be considered as a valuable regulative ideal, radical or total autonomy is an utopia. Contravening what he sees as a polarization posed by Castoriadis, Smith sees relative autonomy as the only realizable form of autonomy that can exist in continuous tension with relative heteronomy.[17] Even though Smith correctly observes that Castoriadis does not pose autonomy as a final state, he reads a false opposition between heteronomy and autonomy.

Klooger (2009, pp. 288–94) also discusses Castoriadis' identification of the emergence of the project of autonomy with democracy and, like Arnason, he sees the invention of democracy as a developmental process where the project of autonomy antecedes the invention of democracy, however imperfectly interpreted. Nevertheless, he acknowledges the ancient Greek polis as unique and finds no historical evidence of similar sanctioned projects of autonomy within the axial civilizations. Klooger sees no previously operating ontological premises that center on conceptions of the self and its nature, origins, capacities, and relations with the world as the ontological conceptions characterized as autonomous by Castoriadis. For Klooger, even though within the axial civilizations there could have been a significant emergence of heterodoxies that made possible the creation of an imaginary conducive to and consistent with a project of autonomy, he acknowledges none within these societies (*ibid.*, p. 293).

Klooger (*ibid.*, p. 292) reasserts the need to differentiate autonomy and heteronomy, distinguishing autonomy from sheer self-reflexivity, not only in terms of the open-ended character of the activities of self-reflection and self-transformation that it involves, but in terms of the self-understanding and intent of these activities. Autonomy cannot be the same everywhere, but this does not mean that any kind of self-reflection qualifies as autonomy. However, he sees a need to moderate heteronomy in view of the observable variation and relativization of social institutions and societies, recognizing differences in the way self-reflexivity can be understood and practiced, triggering new relationships between significations and societies (*ibid.*, p. 315).

I find this last position of Klooger's more consistent with Castoriadis' understanding of the ancient Greek polis and the emergence of philosophy and democracy as germs of autonomy that have to be differentiated as alterity and not merely as different social products of the radical imaginary. Rather than trying to find intercultural or trans-cultural varieties of autonomy projects throughout history, the point here is to pose autonomy as the criterion that allows us to differentiate among social forms, acknowledge discontinuity and rupture within history, and distinguish between closure and openness in a society.

It is imprecise to state that Castoriadis confines history to heteronomy, or to state that he poses polarities in this respect. On the contrary, Castoriadis consistently acknowledges the ever-present tension in society between openness and closure, and the instituted and the instituting. Autonomy and heteronomy are always relative. Heteronomy is, as Klooger correctly puts it, "that what need not to be, in order to be, presents itself as that which could not be otherwise" (*ibid.*, p. 325).

Castoriadis never posed such a thing as total autonomy as a finished model of society, or as an absolute or transcendental condition that emerges out of nothing. The contextual conditions that limit creations such as autonomy are not to be understood as accumulations of events historically experienced in a linear chronology that produce creations or that which are creatively interpreted. To claim that the ancient Greek polis is the germ of autonomy does not mean that it was originated by a certain particular set of events and conditions, or that it reflected a specific interpretation of latent meanings present across cultures. Autonomy has no origin; it is part of the circle of creation within which the instituted and the instituting imaginary of societies create social forms as a mode of being of the social-historical.

Finally, the question about the legitimacy of heterogeneous intercultural forms that ought to be appreciated and valued in their singularity, posed by Arnason, can be answered precisely by Castoriadis' posing of a normative criterion by which to compare and differentiate among diverse societies without falling into cognitive closure or ethnocentric perspectives. The rejection of ethnocentricism is a direct implication of autonomy. It presupposes the anthropological question that stops dividing the world between "us" and "them"; us being the only true human beings, the others being inferior, savage, or barbarian. Autonomy opens up questions about every social institution and prevents a single representation of the world as the only meaningful one. Moreover, autonomy is not a mere western Eurocentric prejudice, even though it arose in the west. For Castoriadis, achieving autonomy means overcoming religious or secular fundamentalisms, forms of messianism, or "idyllic ideas of an Arcadia." It means the access of a large mass of people to a condition of lucid self-reflective thought that permits a common collaboration without the totemization of institutions. This would entail a willful guidance of the polymorphous impulses of psychic chaos toward paths that make life possible and enable self-rule. Furthermore, autonomy implies the capacity to transfer the narcissistic identifications of social groups (that is, societies or nations) to more general identifications, understanding that "the singular human" belongs to humanity (Castoriadis, 2010a, p. 163). Autonomy is the correlate of true politics, philosophy, and a new understanding of democracy.

Autonomy as democracy

An attentive reading of Castoriadis' work reveals a new definition of democracy as the self-institution of society ingrained in his concepts of creation, autonomy, and instituting and instituted powers. The collective dimension of autonomy was linked by Castoriadis to an idea of politics and democracy where society is not frozen in a conception of what is just, equal, or free, but rather institutes itself in such a way that the questions of freedom, of justice, and of equity and equality might be continually reconsidered as part of the "normal" functioning of society (Castoriadis, 1987, p. 87).

Democracy endows an expansive collectivity with increasing creative power where individuals should participate with real conditions—not only formal conditions—to modify the laws and decisions that concern them as social members of a society. Democratic regimes do not presuppose a naturally given collective subject or the idea of popular sovereignty with representative powers. It means the creation of new social forms and institutions through a public sphere where common ends can be articulated despite the multiplicity of subject's positions. Furthermore, it presupposes the constitution of a collective subjectivity capable of bridging different social imaginary significations and different political agendas.

A democratic society should simultaneously separate and articulate the three spheres that Castoriadis described as the social spaces where the relationship of individuals and society are played out: the private sphere (oikos), the public/private sphere (agora), and the public/public sphere (ecclesia).[18] A necessary condition for an autonomous society is that the ecclesia truly be a public space and not merely an object of private appropriation by particular groups. The implications of this condition affect the organization of all power existing in society. It means that "constitutionally" speaking, the legislative, judicial, and governmental powers belong to the people and are exercised by the people (Castoriadis, 1997c, pp. 405–7).

It is with the advent of democracy, as embodying the germ of autonomy in the ancient Greek polis, that the distinction between politics and the political was sanctioned. Castoriadis understands the meaning of politics (*le politique*) as the explicit collective activity that aims at being lucid (reflective and deliberative) and whose object is the institution of society as such. Politics pertains to everything in society that permits participation and that can be shared (Castoriadis, 1991c, pp. 160, 169). Its object is to create the institutions that individuals internalize in order to facilitate their accession to individual autonomy and effective participation in all forms of explicit power in a society. The political (*la politique*), on the other hand, refers to the exercise of explicit power, to the dimension of society pertaining to the existence of institutions capable of formulating explicitly sanctionable injunctions (*Ibid.*, p. 156). It is this distinction that is at stake in the germ of the autonomy project pursued in the ancient Greek polis and democracy.

As Kalyvas (2008, p. 297) has affirmed, by introducing the ideal of political autonomy as collective self-determination Castoriadis moves away from a restrictive and limited definition of democracy as a stable, constitutional, and always already instituted regime that translates itself into a number of criteria, procedures, mechanisms, or forms of legality. Without reducing democracy to juridical forms and rules, democratic legitimacy is grounded on participatory and inclusive attributes of practices, norms, and institutions that have autonomy as a higher foundational principle and evaluative parameter. The transgressive and revolutionary nature of autonomy resides in the recognition that instituted reality does not exhaust and cannot exhaust all forms of political action that emerge at the edges of the instituted nomos.

The ancient Greek creation of democracy is presented as a germ that raised the ongoing question: What is it that the institution of society (i.e., laws, forms of government, etc.) ought to achieve? Inspired by this ancient Greek, Castoriadis favors direct democracy over representative democracy.[19] He sees no "reasonable foundations" to justify an idea of representative democracy that only finds support in a "metaphysics of political representation" (Castoriadis, 1997d, p. 90). Castoriadis questions false assumptions present in representative democracies such as equal participation. He also critics common practices in representative democracies like bureaucratic practices, concentration of power by social elites—usually political parties, monopolies, or bureaucratized bodies that claim to represent collective interests—fictitious separation of powers, the illusion of "experts" being the fittest to "manage" political affairs, and the growing distance between the capacity to attain power and the capacity to govern in today's democracies (2010b, pp. 206–15).

In short, representative democracy holds onto the sophism of full participation and popular sovereignty that, in reality, citizens can only exercise one day every few years, when they elect representatives who actually do not represent them. For this reason, Castoriadis supports direct democracy where a genuine becoming-public of the public/public sphere could take place, enabling the reappropriation of power by the collective through the unfettered circulation of politically pertinent information, the eradication of bureaucracy, the decentralization of decision-making, and the universal participation in decision-making processes (1997c, p. 415).

By direct democracy, Castoriadis does not mean full transparency or the sheer exercise of collective will. It does not relate to a rationalist or a voluntarist utopia. Direct democracy is not a naïve ideal of full popular sovereignty where the demos transparently rules and governs itself, embodying in this way the project of autonomy. It is a mistake to reduce and equate direct democracy to autonomy as Cohen (2005, p. 24) does. Cohen argues that Castoriadis builds two theories of democracy based on different understandings of autonomy, one compatible with the key features of representative government and the other not. In her view this is so because Castoriadis' critical remarks about representative regimes rest on an overly concrete, unmediated, and undifferentiated idea of popular sovereignty.

It is pertinent to bear in mind that popular sovereignty and participation should be understood in light of the project of autonomy where, like the autonomous subject, the democratic subject will never acquire a full identity or exhaust the instituting power. The instituting society can never be fully contained or exhausted by the instituted society. The fully transparent and autonomous society, where the instituted power has totally appropriated the instituting power, would signify the end of history. But the moment of absolute coincidence can never be realized, and we are once again referred to the virtuoso circle of creation where autonomous democracies are created by autonomous subjects, who, in turn, come to be through democratic social institutions that enable autonomy. It is in this sense that for Castoriadis real democracy cannot be limited to institutional and participatory mechanisms that ensure every one's participation—even though it must also guarantee them.

Castoriadis sees direct democracy as enabling more autonomous collectives, where there is no division of political labor between the representative and the represented,[20] given that one can delegate political tasks but not represent or be represented in one's political will. For Castoriadis, institutionalized forms or mechanisms that enable people to manifest their options (i.e., elections, referendums, or plebiscites in representative regimes) are not enough. Institutions and participatory mechanisms must not be fetishized or prevent the conscious appropriation of the instituting power by the collectivity. Changing or qualifying the relation between representatives and the represented, or between representative governments and the discourse of popular sovereignty, as Cohen (2005, p. 32) suggests, are not viable options for him. Castoriadis rules out representation without explaining how this substantial component of modern democracies can be removed from the scale and complexity of contemporary democratic forms of government. Consistent with his position, he refuses to provide models of direct-democratic institutions or forms of government that would produce autonomous individuals and ensure the ceaseless exercise of the instituting imaginary. Ultimately, democracy depends upon an "enormous popular movement" that seeks autonomy brewed through the Paideia(Castoriadis, 2007, p. 74). This can be read as a theoretically consistent but incomplete answer that says everything and nothing.

Nevertheless, despite this just critique, if we agree with Castoriadis that "our problem is to instaurate genuine democracies under contemporary conditions" (Castoriadis, 1997d, p. 99), we must keep in mind that autonomous democracies are conceived as ongoing rather than finished projects, where autonomous positions are relative to its institutions. Following this statement, Mouffe (2007) is correct when she refers to the project of democracy as a horizon that cannot be strictly defined, but which involves new institutions that reflect plurality in society and seek general interests where the common good is to be defined by citizens (Castoriadis, 2007, p. 87). In her view, this might involve a mixed regime of both direct and representative forms of government that would keep autonomy as a foundational and evaluative principle.

I see Mouffe's as the only possible answer to the questions Castoriadis leaves open. However, Castoriadis sheds some light when he cites the rediscovery of direct democracy in modern history in political collective processes of radical self-constitution and self-activity, such as the Paris Commune (1991b, p. 107). It is likewise the case with the green, women's, or youth social movements, which he characterizes as collectivities whose object is explicit self-institution in the attempt to break heteronomy in contemporary democracies. These movements have enlarged the practices of new political wills, expanded the boundaries of political space, and implemented—though often precariously—effective political forms of participation through deliberate collective actions (Castoriadis, 2010c, p. 117). In Kalyvas's (2008, p. 299) words, these could be the voluntary political associations whose collective constitutes the inescapable ground upon which democracy is constructed. These confront us with the ever-present question embedded in the creative and productive character of society: What are the social institutions that under contemporary conditions allow creation to emerge through the incessant activity of the instituting imaginary?

As seen earlier, this question does not have a definite answer, along with other problems that Castoriadis poses before the inherited ontology of being. Characteristically, Castoriadis' thinking sparks challenging queries when elucidating the existing being, and especially when approaching more common and day-to-day issues that involve our quotidian practices within social institutions. Some of these questions might even be seen as inconceivable by the instituted knowledge and our understanding of our primary institutions, such as contemporary democracy. This chapter has discussed some of the debated aspects and critiques made of Castoriadis' arguments. Many of these can be answered or contested by using Castoriadis' arguments. Others—according to some thinkers—remain open and cannot be responded to.

Here I have tried to do justice to the most important critical issues presented in relation to Castoriadis' philosophy. Whether one agrees or not with these discussions, what becomes clear is the original character of Castoriadis' thinking that provides unprecedented and unique ontological explanations, and brings fresh questionings to different orders of knowledge and politics.

A significant contribution of Castoriadis resides in his notion of autonomy and the relationship he establishes with agency to produce an innovative definition of democracy. This presents a different understanding of the normative criteria in the anthropological and political realms, allowing us to redefine democratic social projects and differentiate social and cultural practices without falling into naïve and sometimes perverse relativism. By making this contribution, Castoriadis distances himself from post-structuralist principles that influenced widespread understandings of society, culture, and the subject, such as Foucault's as explained in Chapter 4.

Chapter 4

Michel Foucault: The Game of Power and Resistance

Up to now I have presented Castoriadis' developments, focusing on the notions of the subject, the production of social meaning, and social change. This chapter introduces a dialogue between Castoriadis' theoretical body and Foucault's poststructuralist developments, which has been a far more influential and contemporary corpus in philosophy and social sciences since the 1970s. I first provide a general overview of Foucault's work, illustrating his positions on key notions from the 1960s to the 1980s that will allow a subsequent constructive comparison with Castoriadis. I look at problems that were at the center of Foucault's theory and which shaped the evolution of his work in the poststructuralist intellectual context, such as power, domination, history, and subjectivity.[1] Here, as well as in the next chapter, I intend to see how these problems were differently approached and advanced by Foucault and Castoriadis, pointing out limitations and potentialities of each author in order to create a fruitful debate.

Foucault's work is widely known and has been extensively analyzed in the last thirty years. For this reason I do not intend to make an exhaustive examination of his total intellectual production. As is evident in the following sections, my interpretation of Foucault is limited to the principal questions he shared—independently—with Castoriadis. My analysis of Foucault relies on previous interpretations—in my view, just and accurate—by other scholars who have taken into account a psychoanalytical perspective in their work. Primarily, my arguments follow early writings by Dews (1984, 1987, 1995) and Whitebook (1995, 2005), who show the problems and consequences of the absence of the psychoanalytical perspective for Foucault's theoretical coherence and consistency.

Foucault and Poststructuralism

Despite ambiguities and disagreements in relation to the term poststructuralism, it is possible to say that it is neither a simple rejection nor extension of structuralism, but a series of philosophical reflections on the structuralist program and its failures and achievements. Foucault never accepted being called a poststructuralist, however, along with other authors such as Derrida, he reacted against ontological and epistemological principles that structuralist formalism had inherited from the French intellectual milieu (Merquior, 1986, p. 195).

As with structuralism, the Saussurean legacy made its way into many of the assumptions Foucault relied upon when he was elaborating early concepts such as discourse or episteme. Following the principles of the reflexivity and referentiality of the linguistic sign, he denied a natural preexistence of ideas and objects that were to be named by language; conversely, it was language that created concepts. Poststructuralists came to believe all human systems were socially constructed within a linguistic logic and operated like language. As linguistic productions, the social systems that humans inhabited maintained different and specific meanings and values that structured social life in different cultural and historical formations. In consequence, this principle negated the false ideas of autonomous and natural worlds of meaning and values, where truth or objective reality could be implied.

The fundamental criterion for poststructuralism became the development of an epistemic and evaluative pluralism. Unity and universality were inherently oppressive. Since no conception of truth could ever justify the universal validity that it claimed, such a claim could only mask a desire for power, the wish to unify coercively a multiplicity of standpoints. Truth became an instrument of power. Specifically for Foucault, it necessarily implied domination and unification (Dews, 1987, pp. 217–22).

Following these premises, theoretical activity for poststructuralists could no longer refer to unchanging external absolutes. Such reflexivity always remained tentative, incapable of universal generalization and framed in historical discontinuities. Poststructuralists saw the work of analysis not as linear, but as an assemblage, a pastiche comprising different figures, views, and opinions. In their view, the role of cause or explanation in theory led to evolutionist conclusions and worked against the purposes of what, for example, Foucault called the genealogy of difference, which attempted to establish and preserve the singularity of events. Theory, in Foucault's opinion, should concentrate on the discredited, the neglected, and a whole range of phenomena that had been denied a history. Theory should not have room for constants, essences, or immobile forms of uninterrupted continuities that had structured the past. In this way, rejecting unifying modes of theory as rationalist myths, Foucault and poststructuralists believed it was impossible to know reality itself. Meaning and representation were always shifting and unstable, and the subject, a prisoner of its own discourse, could never know absolute and verifiable contents of reality (Best and Kellner, 1991, pp. 9, 11; Sarup, 1993, p. 59).

Poststructuralists criticized the claim that the mind had innate and universal structures. Instead, they favored a historical view with different forms of consciousness, identities, and signification as historical products that varied over time. However, despite these critiques they retained structuralism's elimination of the subject as the creator of reality. They held antihumanist positions and denied that an individual's intentions, purposes, and goals were products of a free agent who controlled their own actions. The subject as the knowing, willing, autonomous, self-critical, or transcendental ego was put into question and, in consequence, a subject capable of determining truth in a way that associated it with ontological specifications was deemed invalid.

For Foucault, the way the subject was configured within language and systems of meaning and power were constitutive problems. This led him to develop a theory of discourse, which, as mentioned, analyzed subjects, culture, and society as semiotically structured social phenomena. Socially constructed meaning was related to the particularities of institutional sites and practices that were at the heart of the subjective formation of individuals. Discourse was a site and object of struggle, where different groups strove for hegemony and the production of ideology (Best and Kellner, 1991, pp. 20–6; Merquior, 1986, p. 196).

In Foucault's early works the subject was constituted in and through power-discourse formations, and subjectivity was structured under the aegis of a power-discourse matrix. The subject was situated within a social and discursive context and could not be anything but a linguistic possibility, merely a locus of multiple, dispersed, or decentered discourses. Thus for Foucault, as well as for poststructuralists in general, the focus of interest moved away from the subject as such. Given its constitutive role, what became important was to decipher the formation of discourse and its means of power rather than the problems of subject and subjectivity. Transcendentalism was not located in the subject but in the discourse formations, creating in this way a kind of Cartesianism without the subject, as often emphasized.

Following this line of argumentation, two fundamental Enlightenment propositions—the power of reason and the central role of humankind in determining its own destiny and progress—were reconsidered as means of social and political control. Poststructuralists eliminated the principles of moral authority and truth-telling that modernism proclaimed. It undermined the principles of autonomy and the auto-reflexive subject, the emancipatory interest in the past and the future, and the possibility of a political criticism that could go beyond mere immanent social criticism. Social critique had to renounce the normative moment where there would be a distinction between better or worse forms of life.

Foucault's poststructuralist roots

Foucault has been widely recognized as a representative of poststructuralism, because he drew upon an anti-Enlightenment tradition that rejected the equation of reason, emancipation, and progress in arguing that modern forms of power and knowledge have served to create new forms of domination. However as noted, he always rejected this identification (Foucault, 1983a, p. 198).

Foucault abandoned certain aspects of structuralist analysis that dealt with the elimination of notions of meaning and the conception of a formal model of human behavior as rule-governed transformations of meaningless elements. He also sought to avoid both the phenomenological project of tracing all meaning back to the meaning-giving activity of an autonomous, transcendental subject, and the attempt to read off the implicit meaning of social practices as a hermeneutical exercise (Dreyfus and Rabinow, 1983, p.xxiv).

Foucault concentrated on different problems as time passed. Foucault's early works were concerned with the relationships and forces that constituted a subject, rather than with a subject whose reason and agency constituted knowledge and endowed the world with meaning. In time, Foucault moved from a more linguistic and determinant analysis to one where power relationships were seen as an ultimate principle of social reality. Power was seen by Foucault to be everywhere and not exclusively invested in the central organizing institutions, such as the state.

During the mid 1960s his attention was directed almost exclusively toward the history of discursive formation and its relationship with knowledge and power. For most of the 1970s, however, the autonomy of discourse was blurred and dissolved, and he saw epistemic structures as completely molded by social forces. Finally, in his late work, the problem of the subject—which had long been viewed as an effect or a construct—emerged and Foucault became interested in the modalities of moral self-constitution and in what he termed as "aesthetics of existence." This evolution in Foucault's work has been seen by some authors as an internal contradiction, which at one stage lead to an announcement of the "death of man," while at a later stage Foucault advocated the promotion of new forms of subjectivity which required a previous theoretical notion of the subject (Williams, 2001, pp. 152–89; Dews, 1987, p. 232).

Initially, in *The Order of Things* (1966), Foucault sought to explain the emergence of social sciences, their relationship with power, and the way knowledge was historically produced and value charged through the concepts of episteme and discourse. Episteme evidenced the systemic nature of all knowledge and referred to the structures of thought that typify the thinking of a particular age. A particular episteme is always bound to give rise to a particular form of knowledge, he claimed. The term "discourse" referred to the accumulation of social practices (moral, domestic, political, reproductive, economic, and intellectual), concepts, statements, and beliefs that were produced by a particular episteme. It could be understood as practices that systematically form the objects of which they spoke. Discourse was both the production of a statement and its social status, including its institutional setting; it was desire and power already in action (Foucault, 1970; 1972, p. 138).

These two notions allowed Foucault to redirect his thinking away from modernist ideas about truth or reality, showing how a historically specific system of norm-governed social practices defined and produced each epoch's distinctive subjects and objects of knowledge and power. In consequence, he proposed a new kind of historiography—first called archeology, then genealogy—that could chart the emergence and disappearance of such systems of practice and describe their specific function (Fraser, 1989, p. 38).

Based on these principles, Foucault developed new conceptions about global and totalizing forms of knowledge, truth, history, continuity, and discontinuity.[2] His work attempted to break down the theoretical forms of analysis, history, and society as unified wholes governed by a center, essence, or telos. Foucault stood against universalism and saw theory and history as nonevolutionary and fragmented. He stated that no past era could be understood purely in its own terms, given that history was, in a sense, always a history of the present. Historicism therefore represented a danger.

This was intimately related to what Foucault understood as truth. History and knowledge were intimately related to what truth represented in its relative nature and character. Culturally and historically constructed, truth was defined within different epistemes and/or power regimes. Foucault insisted that all regimes of power were also regimes of truth constituted by a system of ordered procedures for the production, regulation, distribution, circulation, and operation of statements. Truth was defined as having a circular relation with systems of control that produced and sustained it, and with the effects of power that it induced and which in turn extended it (Foucault, 1980, p. 133). Given the existence of different regimes of truth and their relativity, it followed that no historical period or society could be judged as better than others. Foucault himself recognized that what he had written was merely fiction, acknowledging that there existed the possibility for fiction to function in truth, or for fictional discourse to induce effects of truth (*ibid.*, pp. 143–4).

With this rationale, Foucault did not approach truth from a perspective of formal criteria and logical coherence. Instead he was interested in questions such as: Who is able to tell the truth? What are the moral and ethical conditions that entitle one to present oneself as a truth speaker? And what is the relationship between truth telling and the exercise of power? (Rabinow, 1994, p. 204).

Foucault's concern was with the history of the relationships that thought maintained with truth. He stated that far from the concept of truth implying domination and forcible unification, it was precisely contempt for truth that characterized the arbitrary use of political power. At the base of this was the characteristic poststructuralist resistance to the standpoint of totalization, which was understood as repressive. In Foucault's view, totalizing represented "an attempt to reveal determinations, and in so doing appropriate the truth content of all other partial standpoints, on the basis of an anticipation of a future nonantagonistic society" (Dews, 1987, p. 201).

As noted, Foucault read humanism from this perspective, equating it to a political rhetoric and practice that developed at the beginning of the modern era in order to oppose what were essentially premodern forms of domination and oppression. Foucault saw the modern subject as a humanist fiction and was critical of the philosophical tradition that took for granted that human subjects were self-reflexive, responsible, and autonomous. In his view, the notion of autonomy was unrelated to the critical capacity of judgment, and having a humanist position was not a prerequisite for critically approaching social institutions, social relationships, prisons, social science, or sexuality. The notion of critical thinking was grounded and constructed around the idea of resistance to oppressive social forms and relations. Social criticism did not arise from the qualities and conditions that enabled individuals to interrogate and change their own ways of being based on normative criteria that established differences among cultural practices.

Foucault developed these general considerations through his various projects. Over time, his work transformed in some of its basic notions, but maintained a vivid theoretical activity that innovatively questioned and analyzed forms of power present in modern Western societies.

Early and Late Foucault: From Archaeology to the Technologies of the Self

Early works: Foucault's archaeology of knowledge

In 1961 Foucault became known in Paris with the publication of *Madness and Civilization*. In this book he showed how madness and "unreason" were conceived in the seventeenth and eighteenth centuries, and why those conceptions differed from other ways of understanding madness in other historical periods. Foucault saw reason and madness as phenomena that resulted from historical processes, and not as universal or objective categories. Using this case he illustrated the way epistemes worked, describing how madness, poverty, and unemployment began to be perceived as social problems. The meaning and ethical values linking them determined the way these phenomena were experienced in this epoch (Foucault, 1973a, pp. 38–64).

Writing the history of madness meant carrying out a structural study of the historical ensemble—notions, institutions, and juridical and scientific measures—that socially created the madness phenomenon within a context where irrational (mad) and rational individuals were recognized and differentiated. In this work Foucault was also concerned with the transformation of the structures of experience through which humans became able to think of themselves as the subjects of purely procedural rationality, and to consider other "irrational" human beings as the possible objects of enquiry. For Foucault, freedom of the rational self was not impaired by the irruption of madness. Instead, madness was stripped of its powers and prestige through the formation of rational awareness, making it a new object of knowledge (*ibid.*, pp. 241–78; Dews, 1984, p. 89).

Foucault explained the emergence of madness as a mode of becoming, through a discursive formation, a type of subject that had not existed previously. His target was not the study of madness as a social phenomenon, but its scientific categorization and the social conditions that permitted such labeling and value charging. Madness was an example of a mode of objectification that transformed human beings into subjects, and simultaneously created institutions that encompassed, sustained, and reproduced them as subjects (Foucault, 1983b, p. 208).

Likewise, Foucault stressed the institutional and political preconditions for the elaboration of a form of knowledge in *The Birth of the Clinic* (1963). In this case, the science in question was one of the body rather than of the mind. Foucault analyzed the shift from a premodern medicine to modern, rationalized, empirically based medicine. He argued that modern medical experience suffered a reformulation where diseases were connoted and medically classified using mechanisms that marked the concrete space of the body (1973b, p. 16).

In these two first books, Foucault set up the bases of his work on knowledge, social practices, and power. Deepening his interest, in 1966 he published *The Order of Things*. There he focused on the plane of representation, revealing the mode of constructing and naming the objects of knowledge that produced meaning, subjectivity, and signification. His aim was to show key elements in power relations and their domination effects, and illustrate the conflict within which discourses emerged and functioned.

Knowledge inflicted discipline, surveillance, and regulation. This could be seen in certain empirical forms of knowledge such as psychiatry. Knowledge disciplines constructed different ways of seeing or speaking about their object, delimiting its boundaries to define what was true or false. Foucault saw this same principle working in all social representations. He showed how the mode of representation that existed in the medieval and classical ages contrasted with the modern age, where discourse and language gave birth to the subject as an epistemological category. As is widely known, Foucault stated that before the eighteenth century, man did not exist as any more than the potency of life and the productivity of labor. He wrote that man was quite a recent creature (1970, p. 308). He stated:

> What is available to archaeological analysis is the whole of Classical knowledge or rather the threshold that separates us from Classical thought and constitutes modernity. It was upon this threshold that the strange figure of knowledge called man first appeared and revealed a space proper to the human sciences (*ibid.*, p. xxiv).

By using the term "man" to denote subjectivity as the source and locus of mental representations of reality, he endorsed the structuralist elimination of the central role given to subjectivity. In this sense social sciences illustrated how man could be both the constituting source of the world's meaning and, at the same time, just another natural object in the world. At this time, Foucault praised Levi-Strauss' anthropology and psychoanalysis because, in his view, only they were able to explain consciousness and its representations of the world in terms of more fundamental principles. Though he later modified this position, especially toward psychoanalysis, initially Foucault defended the idea that these disciplines provided descriptions of psychological and cultural structures that were not themselves representational but that which explained the functioning of conscious representations (*ibid.*, pp. 373–87; Gutting, 1994, pp. 11–12).

In effect, Foucault followed this structuralist view, seeing the cogito as an outmoded form of thought and showing that there was no subject or object that was not constructed by a discursive formation. As in structuralism, he believed that the epistemological appeal to a reality or principle outside discourse lacked any sense. For him, it was impossible to step outside of discourse in order to compare discursive representations with something other than themselves. As stated by Dews (1987, p. 184) and Jameson (1972, pp. 192–216) this illustrated how, rather than supporting the transcendence of the subject, Foucault supported the transcendence of discourse without the subject.

In *The Order of Things*, as well as in his later work *The Archaeology of Knowledge* (1969), the center of Foucault's attention became discursive practices and the rules that guided them. He called this archaeology, stating:

> It is these rules of formation, which were never formulated in their own right, but are to be found only in widely differing theories, concepts, and objects of study, that I have tried to reveal, by isolating, as a specific locus, a level that I call archaeology (1970, pp. xi, 13).

For Foucault these rules did not confer upon discourse a priori conditions for rational operations; they had no transcendental status, nor were they claimed to be external to discourse or to prefigure it. He thought of these rules, which he later called operations of power, as modes of experience, systems of meaning, and objects of knowledge. The role of the archeologist was to examine discourses as practices that obeyed certain rules. The function of archaeology was to see how enunciative modalities made it possible to speak of the subject and how discourses spoke through subjects. It referred to the subject who was inserted in the field of possible enunciations, to the position of the subject established by a discursive formation (Foucault, 1972, pp. 138–40).

Drawing on the rules of discourse, Foucault worked on the conception of a new history that was challenging ideas of continuity and totality. Foucault wrote: "A total description draws all phenomena around a single center—a principle, a meaning, a spirit, a world view, an overall shape; a general history, on the contrary, would deploy the space of a dispersion" (*ibid.*, pp. 5–10). Based on his argument about the historical contingency of knowledge, he exemplified how the discourses that dictated the system of order in the middle and classical ages could be seen as temporary epistemological arrangements. The term discontinuity referred to processes of transition from one historical era to another, in which things were no longer perceived, described, characterized, and classified in the same way (Foucault, 1970, p. 50). Discontinuity could be seen, for example, in Foucault's work on madness. For this reason, the archaeologist's method was to find discontinuities within the multiplicity of discourses in a field of knowledge: "archaeology does not have a unifying but a diversifying effect" (Foucault, 1972, p. 160). However, the ruptures that made possible this discontinuity, or transition from one episteme to another, were not given in a vacuum. Foucault argued that these ruptures were possible on the basis of the rules that were in operation. Discontinuity meant not absolute change, but a redistribution of the episteme's elements. It was not about the instauration of new rules, but a discursive formation upon which truth and knowledge redefined its boundaries. Such ruptures maintained certain continuity and overlapping in the transition from modern science to counter-sciences, where the importance of the problem of representation remained at the center of the discussion.

What interested Foucault was opening the structures to temporal discontinuity and showing shifts that determined the endless game of discursive practices. Deconstructing history was part of the work of the new historians that involved abandoning the search for continuity. As some authors have put it, this principle resembled the structuralist perspective that involved affirming that history was marked by gradual effacement of discourse (Best and Kellner, 1991, p. 44; Dosse, 1997, pp. 238–9 (vol. 2)). This standpoint affirmed the predominance of discourse over history. In history, different forms of knowledge were equated to different perspectives, recognizing in this way the impossibility of historical objective knowledge and historical continuity. History introduced discontinuity into our very being, disrupting its pretended continuity (Foucault, 1977, p. 154; 1972, pp. 130–1).

Along with his early work on epistemic ruptures, Foucault theorized relationships with power as the causal factors that lead from one episteme to another. Even though in *The Order of Things* and *The Archaeology of*

Knowledge his emphasis was on knowledge and scientific discourses, he had already begun to explore the relationship of power to these phenomena. As early as *The Birth of Clinic*, he was concerned with policing, surveillance, and disciplinary apparatus. Later, Foucault's explicit recognition of the relationship of power to knowledge presented power as a precondition of knowledge, rather than vice versa, which had important consequences for his understanding of the social sciences. The mutations in different epistemes that he addressed suggested the effect of power in the generation of new kinds of subjects and new organizations of relationships between individuals and institutions. These observations were most explicitly developed in *Discipline and Punish* (1975), where he worked with the connections between modern methods of social control (such as the prison) and the emergence of criminology and related social sciences.

At the end of the 1960s, when the wave of structuralism began to subside, discourse ceased being the most important issue in Foucault's work, and power and its technologies of the body acquired greater relevance. He abandoned the notion of the episteme and moved to a genealogical perspective, an important shift from the archaeologist's approach. In 1970 he began to make this transition through a more focused theorization of material institutions and forms of power. He placed more emphasis on the material conditions of discourse, defining them as institutions, political events, and economic practices (Foucault, 1972, p. 49).

This genealogical orientation inspired Foucault's publications of the midseventies that brought the body into his analysis. Here he looked at the relationships between power, knowledge, and the body in modern society. Through genealogy, Foucault tried to widen his scope of analysis, centering on forms of control that targeted the body and its consequences on individual subjectivity. These inquiries, which characterized Foucault's work in the 1970s and 1980s, introduced a new set of conceptions and problems.

Foucault's genealogical approach to power

During 1970s the genealogical perspective that Foucault adopted gave more importance to discipline and sexuality and their relations to the human body. Foucault directed his genealogical investigation with the intention of locating the political effects of discourse on the human body. He saw the body as invested in, governed by, and transformed by specific power relationships. Through genealogy he studied the power processes of institutional practices within which objects and subjectivities were created. Genealogy was used to unveil the material context of the construction of the subject, in an attempt to see the political consequences of this subjectification while focusing on the effects of control (Foucault, 1980, pp. 83–5; Dreyfus and Rabinow, 1983, p. 104; Best and Kellner, 1991, p. 47).

Discipline and Punish considered the specific case of the connection between modern social scientific disciplines and the disciplinary practices used to control human bodies in the modern period. This was exemplified in the practice of imprisonment, as conceived by criminology and other social scientific disciplines that dealt with crime and punishment (for example, social psychology) (Foucault, 1979, pp. 231–56). Practices such as torture and the regulation of prisoners, exercised in institutions such as hospitals or barracks, were mechanisms of surveillance, which was thought to be efficient and profitable when it came to managing a population. Surveillance acted as an inside eye, having the same effect as the panopticon or the Freudian super-ego (*ibid.*, pp. 195–228).

Foucault shifted his emphasis to processes of corporeal regulation and control that gave rise to bodies of knowledge about the objects they controlled. He wanted to illustrate how relationships of power produced forms of subjectivity through techniques of normalization. Having begun to address this in his earlier work, Foucault reaffirmed that power and knowledge directly implied one another, holding a relationship of mutual dependence and reinforcement (*ibid.*, p. 27). Knowledge could not exist independently of power: their deployment was simultaneous. He stated:

It is not the activity of the subject of knowledge, that produces a corpus of knowledge, useful or resistant to power, but power-knowledge, the processes and struggles that traverse it and of which it is made up, which determines the forms and possible domains of knowledge (*ibid.*, p. 28).

Despite the fact that becoming an object of knowledge represented a form of domination for Foucault (Foucault, 1983a), power and domination also implied creating new domains of knowledge and practice. Power, rather than being merely repressive, was also productive; therefore, from this perspective power could be seen as producing realities, domains of truth, and new objects of knowledge. Power was not located in any single site; it was dispersed throughout the social system. Differential power relationships manifested in every aspect of cultural and political life, involving all kinds of subject-positions inducing effects that were not possible for knowledge to engender. Power was not theorized as a group of institutions and mechanisms that ensured the subservience of individuals. Its exercise was not violent nor was it by consent. It was a total structure of actions that incited, induced, and seduced (Foucault, 1978, p. 92).

Individuals were the vehicles and aim of power, since they were constituted by the force of its infliction. In assuming subject-positions, both dominators and subjugators were caught within the same matrix of power relationships.

Power was a strategic, mobile, fluid, and continuous relationship. It invested institutions and individuals with possibilities for action. It was never stationary but was already present in a matrix of forces which itself created lines of division, relationships of exclusion, codes of discipline, and sites of subjection (*ibid.*, pp. 92–102).

The term "bio-power", which Foucault coined in *The History of Sexuality* Vol. I (1978) was based on the conception of power being dispersed, fluid, indeterminate, and productive of individual's bodies, identities, and institutions (*ibid.*, pp. 140–1, 143). Bio-power referred to a power over life, the power to administer the life of individuals and control in general. It targeted new objects of knowledge such as sexuality, objectifying them as resources to be administered and controlled. Foucault stated:

> If we can apply the term of bio-history to the pressures through which the movements of life and the processes of history interfere with one another, one would have to speak of bio-power to designate what brought life and its mechanisms into the realm of explicit calculations and made knowledge-power an agent of transformation of human life (*ibid.*, p. 143).

This problem was extensively worked out in *The History of Sexuality*. Here Foucault presented a genealogical critique of social systems during the seventeenth and eighteenth centuries, as well as their consolidation in modern technological programs of demographic administration and control, with sexuality at the center of the analysis. Sexuality was treated as a positive product of power acting through its repression. Polymorphous techniques of power were inscribed in the body through the discourse of modern sexuality. Science maintained the role of control and normalization and reinforced the medicalization of sexuality (*ibid.*, pp. 10–13, 129–31).

Here again Foucault returned to the idea of discourse production in order to illustrate the emergence of new social forms, in this case the "sexual nature" of humans, and its regulation. He wrote: "The deployment of sexuality has its own reason for being, not in reproducing itself, but in proliferating, innovating, annexing, creating, and penetrating bodies in an increasingly detailed way, and controlling populations in an increasingly comprehensive way" (*ibid.*, p. 107).

Nevertheless, as noted, Foucault was also aware of the forces that opposed power, characterizing these forces as a multiple and mobile field of relationships among forces where far-reaching but never completely stable effects of domination were produced (*ibid.*, p. 102). Where there was power there was resistance and, therefore, the possibility to modify the grip of power through resistance (Foucault, 1988b, p. 123). Foucault used the notion of resistance to designate the way in which individuals could contest and even provoke certain changes in attitudes and practices within established power regimes and social orders, for example, through his concept of counter-discourses, which materialized and expressed ways of resistance to power. By criticizing the institutions that appeared to be neutral and independent, and unmasking the type of domination they exercised, Foucault also illustrated how power confronted contestation and change: it produced reverse discourses, as in the case of homosexuality in relation to modern sexuality, or strategies to counter discipline and normalization.

The ways societies and individuals contested power and escaped impositions of discourse and knowledge over their individuality and desires was a central question throughout Foucault's work. As Dews (1984, 1987) and Best and Kellner (1991) have suggested, Foucault tried to respond more extensively to this question in his later writings by changing his emphasis to the technologies of the self—the ways individuals transformed themselves—and putting aside his interest in the technologies of domination (the way power was inflicted by some individuals on others).

The early weight given in his studies to the technologies of domination and the way those technologies classified, objectified, and normalized subjects, shifts in *The History of Sexuality* (vols. 2 and 3) and other works published in 1980s. Rather than focusing so much on the way society molded individuals through power mechanisms, he became more involved with the way individuals formed their own identity and subjectivity in response to changing power and truth regimes.

This shift aroused new questions and topics in relation to subjectivity, the implicit relationship between society and individuals, mechanisms of change, forms of social criticism, and politics in general. Some of his last works addressed these topics in a new and different way, generating a controversy in relation to his earlier positions.

Last works of Foucault

During the 1980s Foucault's attention moved from the genealogical focus on modalities of power to focus on technologies of the self, ethics, and freedom. Foucault spoke of different types of technologies: technologies of production, which permitted individuals to produce, transform, or manipulate things; technologies of sign systems, which permit us to use signs, meanings, symbols, or signification; technologies of power, which determine the conduct of individuals and submit them to certain ends or domination; and technologies of the self (Foucault, 1988c, p. 18).

Technologies of the self became the most important focus of his work. He defined these as practices that permitted individuals to effect, by their own means or with the help of others, a certain number of operations on their own bodies and souls, thoughts, conduct, and ways of being, so as to transform themselves in order to attain a certain state of happiness, purity, wisdom, perfection, or immortality (*ibid.*, p. 18). Using this concept, Foucault addressed Greek, Roman, and Christian cultures of antiquity in the last two volumes of *The History of Sexuality* (1984). Beginning with early Christian cultures, he demonstrated how the self was a constituted subject of desire. Following this process, he traced the moral dimensions of Christian, Greek, and Roman cultures and the differences among them. He was interested in showing how Greeks and Romans conceived and regulated pleasure and desire through institutions such as marriage, hetero-and homosexuality, and forms of the care of the self. Foucault saw Christianity as closer to modern culture than to that of the Greeks or Romans, which shared their ways of experiencing the body and its potential expressions of beauty without appealing to ethical interdictions. He identified in Christianity the abandonment of a more ethical and aesthetic perspective toward sexuality in favor of a hermeneutics of desire, where individuals sought in sexuality the truth of their being. He believed that Greeks and Romans followed a freer pattern than Christians did in terms of their forms of ethics. In his view, the way Greeks related to the self was more reflexive, and society placed a great emphasis on the responsibility of auto-regulation and the expectation that one is the master of one's own desires. In other words, contrary to the Christian tradition, Greeks and Romans (excepting slaves and women) followed an auto-deliberative schema (Foucault, 1985, pp. 78–93).

Within this analysis Foucault attempted to produce a genealogy of subjectivity. He became increasingly interested in the individual's capacity for self-reflecting and articulating his experience. Foucault used notions such as the aesthetic that opened up the choice of the individual. The aesthetics of existence related to a way of life whose moral value did not depend on a code of behavior, but on certain principles in the use of pleasure (*ibid.*, pp. 89–93). In this way, Foucault showed how Greeks and Romans emphasized their own self-direction, following or modifying what was given as a rule or imposition. This observation marked for Foucault a substantial change with respect to his perception of the auto-deliberative and self-governing subject.

In his later works, Foucault evoked a privatistic realm that allowed the individual to self-reflect and make political decisions. This was also illustrated in his text "What is Enlightenment?" originally published in 1984, where he stated the necessity to analyze individuals as historical products who should orient themselves toward self-constitution as autonomous subjects (1984, p. 43). This echoed what Foucault also declared in a 1983 interview, where he expressed his desire to deal with the analysis of reflexivity—a relationship of self to self—and, hence, of relationships between forms of reflexivity and the discourse of truth, forms of rationality, and the effects of knowledge (1983a, p. 203).

Individualization was no longer a one-sided process that was merely the effect of power. In a positive evaluation of the individual cultivation of the self, the question became the constituting process of individual subjectivity. He wrote:

> Perhaps I've insisted too much on the technologies of domination and power. I am more and more interested in the interaction between oneself and others and the technologies of individual domination, the history of how an individual acts upon himself, in the technologies of the self (1988, p. 19).

He added: "now I am interested, in fact, in the way in which the subject constitutes himself in an active fashion, by the practices of self" (1994, p. 11).

This interest has been interpreted as the shift in Foucault's focus as he departed from subjects dominated and objectified by others through discourses and practices (technologies of domination), to subjects who created their own identities through ethics (technologies of the self) (Dews, 1989). In this line of thinking, Foucault also reevaluated the Enlightenment as a positive contribution to a critical position toward social practices (Foucault, 1984, pp. 32–50). In reconsidering the concept of the subject that he had rejected in his antihumanist work, he started using words such as freedom and autonomy, which could only be coherent with a type of subject that he had never considered before. Foucault's late emphasis on subjectivity confirmed his interest in power, but in a more liberating way with which individuals could transform their own subjectivities. He wrote:

> The political, ethical, social, and philosophical problem of our days is . . . to liberate us both from the state and the type of individualization which is linked to the state. We have to promote new forms of subjectivity through the refusal of this kind of individuality which has been imposed upon us for several centuries (1983b, p. 216).

The shifts in regard to the subject and subjectivity, autonomy, freedom, and political resistance generated incoherencies and problems within Foucault's theoretical trajectory. As Dews (1989, 1987) expressed, Foucault could not develop coherent notions of the subject's autonomy or emancipation without having worked through a different theory in his previous thinking on subject formation. Foucault, through his lifetime work, had theorized the subject as entirely constructed through social practices without developing a solid theory of individual subjectification, which made him unable to conceive emancipation coherently.

In his later development Foucault worked with a notion of the subject that implied dimensions and aspects for which he had no ultimate explanation. When talking about the processes of generating different subjectivities, Foucault needed theoretical tools that were not available in his earlier work. Interrelated problems that were intrinsic to his subjectivity and subjectification concerns were now unresolved and had no satisfactory explanations. The early socialization and subjectification processes which an individual must undergo in order to become a member of society; the subject's internalization of social practices that culture imposes; and the necessary privatistic and reflexive dimension that the individual requires for a critical auto-examination of societal contents—these were all problems that had never been worked out by the author theoretically. To talk about a process that would free the individual from social constraints to become more autonomous, required theoretical tools that Foucault never elaborated.

In Dews' eyes, it was impossible not to read Foucault's later work as ambiguous in relation to power and emancipation, where his task was to articulate the concepts of subjectivity and freedom in such a way as to avoid any suggestion that such freedom had to have taken the form of the recovery of an authentic natural self (Dews, 1989, pp. 38–40).

This evident problem consequently affected Foucault's consistency in previous assertions about meaning and social change. As will be examined in detail in Chapter 5, when reviewed through Castoridian principles, Foucault's positions reveal unresolved questions regarding the three central notions on which we concentrate our comparison. Furthermore, Foucault's late turn can be seen as having an effect on constitutive issues in his work such as power, history, discontinuity, and transformation, while the Castoridian perspective poses interesting and elucidating questions for a better understanding of such notions as will be discussed in the following section and Chapter 5.

Power/Knowledge, History, and Transformation

As described in previous sections, both Castoriadis and Foucault saw a need for groundbreaking critical thinking that distanced them from the theoretical influences of their formative years. Even though Foucault followed a very different trajectory from that of Castoriadis in relation to Marxism, he neither subscribed to Marxist ideas[3] nor entirely engaged structuralist principles. Nor did he fit into other trends of the moment such as phenomenology or existentialism. Foucault's work of social criticism involved new ways of looking at traditional problems, offering innovative interpretations of knowledge, social practices, and society.

His success in configuring an influential field of production, selecting new objects of inquiry, and setting research agendas lies in his unique way of relating issues of domination, governmentality, and subjectivity as articulated by social institutions at different points in time. Foucault's extraordinary ability to illustrate these components as they manifested in specific historical formations and discourses has precipitated readers to identify themselves as social products of relative and conditional dominant forms that shaped their subjective contents, bodies, and daily practices. The exercise of power is in fact his greatest pole of attraction.

As seen, for Foucault power was everywhere and not exclusively invested in central organizing institutions. It was the driving force of society and social transformations: humanity moved from domination to domination throughout time (Foucault, 1977, p. 140). Honneth (1998, p. 158) was right to confirm how for Foucault all historical processes were a succession of forms of domination, despite his different conceptions over time. Knowledge production and strategies of power were his central referents by which to judge history, even when his interest moved from the genesis of the concept of subjectivity to modern representations of the subject and morality. Foucault's theory of power—Honneth added—"regards the production of knowledge and the exercise of domination simply as different sides of the same process [successfully combining] the goal of a history of institutions with the goal of conceptual history" (1998, p. 158).

Discipline and Punish and *The History of Sexuality* confirm this, illustrating simultaneously how modern forms of control also shaped modes of conduct and forms of operation, as well as subjectivities and corporeal realities. Nevertheless, historical accounts successfully used by Foucault to develop his arguments did not escape functionalism. As Honneth stated (1998, pp. 163, 165), Foucault argued in favor of a historically guided functionalism that regarded traditions, ideas, and values only from the perspective of the function they performed in a systematic process characterized by the increase or the use of power; in other words, analyzing social processes as they maximized control or preformatted power over society.

This is true for the distinct interpretations of historical moments and institutions Foucault made. The way this author understood historical discontinuity depended on the emergence and disappearing of systems of practices where their social function becomes a clear criterion that defines historical ruptures. As interested as he was in contesting modernist views of historical continuity, and therefore redefining historical discontinuity and dispersion, Foucault links these last two concepts to transitional epistemological arrangements that through discourse change the way the social is perceived or valued. But despite these changes, the predominance of discourse over history can be found throughout Foucault's work and together with it, the predominance of power.

Both permanency and change are simultaneously present in what he called the ruptures of epistemes or the emergence of new genealogies. Even though the work of the historian is to find discontinuities within the multiplicity of discourses, Foucault defends at the same time the prevalence of discourse and its controlling power as a constant throughout history. A permanent essence of power is invariable and continuous, despite changes in the way institutions and practices represent it throughout time. Even though for Foucault different forms of domination can be identified in historical changes, the essential character of power persists and is just deployed in a different form. In this sense, it becomes hard to sustain that historical ruptures or discontinuities are in essence a mere repetition.

Though this argument against Foucault is valid, it could also be said that it responds to one of Foucault's main goals: theorizing power and its effects on social relationships, institutions, and individuals within a new understanding of history. Opting for a reading that sees Foucault just as a theorist of power—as he has been regarded and praised by many—we need to recognize his originality and refinement when scrutinizing historical formations and their expressions of power. In this sense, Foucault does a greater job than Castoriadis, who never so meticulously dissected power and its modes of being in specific SIS or social institutions.

As seen in previous chapters, one of Castoriadis' main priorities is giving an exhaustive theoretical account of social institutions. Nevertheless, power and domination remain tacit elements that are not his main theoretical concerns. When comparing Foucault and Castoriadis in this respect their differences become evident in the level of abstraction each author used to approach the established relationship between subjects and society. While

Castoriadis' elaboration on social institutions responds to an ontological question, Foucault rejected this stand, opting to elaborate a strategic knowledge based on a piece-by-piece analysis of power—as he described it—rather than on a comprehensive, global, or totalizing explanation of social institutions that promoted modernist ideals (Foucault, 1980, p. 140).

For Castoriadis power is always present in social life and is reflected in social institutions and SIS,[4] however, it is far from being an omnipresent and pervasive element. Despite his reflections upon the existing relationship between subjectivity, subordination, and prevailing and governing SIS, power and domination are not conceptual instruments that Castoriadis finds as potentially explanatory in themselves. Though they play a relevant role in developing important notions such as autonomy, he does not discuss them in depth as specific problems. One could argue that power and domination in Castoriadis are somehow over shadowed throughout his work; however, this is not to say that he is totally foreign to this discussion. The most specific conceptual term he uses to explain these issues is heteronomy, a term he introduced early on as alienation (1987, pp. 108–10) and later formalized as heteronomy, defined vis-à-vis autonomy. Nonetheless, Castoriadis' notion of heteronomy can be blamed for not having been more elaborated or systematically applied into specific social institutions. In this respect, Foucault's mastery at examining techniques of control and the effects of power are greater than Castoriadis' and offer tremendous potentiality. In the eyes of some critics, Castoriadis lacks a thorough analysis of this kind.

Kalyvas (2002, p. 77) stated that Castoriadis' notion of heteronomy remains superficial, limited, and derivative, which weakened his political project. His understanding of heteronomy prevents him from giving a solid account of different forms of domination and asymmetrical power relations. Kalyvas added that Castoriadis' critical views on issues such as capitalism, liberalism, and the state remain somehow dispersed and incomplete, meaning by this that Castoriadis does not elaborate a refined and systematic account of fundamental institutions where social injustice is perpetrated by the imposition of powerful agents and unequal relationships. This judgment is valid despite the fact that Castoriadis does make partial efforts in his later writings to approach critiques of the state, capitalism, religion, and racism in more simple language and pragmatic terms.[5]

Castoriadis' theoretical instruments allow us to identify how the instituted dimension may hamper and constrain, through the effects of power, the creative capacity of individuals and societies. However, he does not undertake a detailed analysis of their modes of operating or make descriptive accounts of power.

Heteronomy, for Castoriadis, might be found in the instituted dimension of society, through which society survives and preserves itself. Domination is expressed in the social closure of heteronomous forms like religion. However, contrary to Foucault, domination is not omnipresent in the instituted, or better put, the instituted is not only domination. Negative effects of domination come into play when instituted SIS or social institutions obscure and obstruct the instituting imaginary and its potential to put into question oneself and one's own society. Castoriadis writes:

> To abolish heteronomy does not signify abolishing the difference between instituting society and instituted society—which, in any case, would be impossible—but to abolish the *enslavement* of the former to the latter. The collectivity will give itself its rules, knowing that *it itself* is giving them to *itself*, that these rules are or will always become at some point inadequate, that it can change them—and that they bind it so long as it has not changed them in a *regular way* (1993a, p. 330).

Indeed, as previously explained, it is the appropriation and exercise of the instituting power by society that enables in Castoriadis the production of new institutions and social imaginary significations. By contrast, for Foucault what triggers the struggle against power and the transformation of institutions is resistance and its productive character that it expresses within ongoing struggles that both maintain and destabilize forms of domination.

What is shared by the instituting imaginary in Castoriadis and the resistance to power in Foucault is their capacity to question existing social forms and generate new and different ones. For both Castoriadis and Foucault these driving forces of change are socially constitutive and individuals and collectives need them to transform what is normalized and naturalized by society. Furthermore, both thinkers emphasize the collective and anonymous character of these changing faculties. For them these come from below and are simultaneously everywhere and nowhere, dispersed and inflicted from innumerable points, and at play in every individual. Transformation is not attributed to a specific or privileged social actor, in order to avoid any essentialization of a class or identity as the unique bearer of justice or wisdom.

Like in Foucault, historical rupture in Castoriadis is related to effects of domination and power. Though explained through very different concepts, collective change in Castoriadis is linked to his concepts of heteronomy and autonomy, as well as to the instituted and the instituting power or imaginary. The most important dimension of historical change that Castoriadis is interested in theorizing has to do with the exercise of the collective instituting power that has brought about autonomous institutions such as philosophy or democracy. Rather than concentrating so much on the historical course of what Castoriadis sees as heteronomous institutions throughout history, he is interested in conceptualizing historical discontinuity on the bases of his notion of autonomy. Discontinuity in history is seen by Castoriadis in the creation of a new eidos, most importantly in the creation of autonomous forms that overcome heteronomous states or forms of societies. It is in this collective potentiality and capacity where Castoriadis sees discontinuity. Contrary to what Foucault sees as repetitious expressions of power throughout history, Castoriadis wants to theorize the break of heteronomy by posing his idea of autonomous creation.

In their respective formulations it is possible to see how Foucault and Castoriadis intended to overcome ideas of history and change that defended ultimate social forms or involved a natural transcendental telos inspired by rationalist, modernist, or liberal views. However, it is apposite to observe central differences in these readings.

As argued earlier, Foucault's position contained functionalist and determinist traits related to power that affect the efficacy of his critical views, his account of history, and his sense of social and individual transformation. Despite his originality and sophistication Foucault was unable to theoretically substantiate his critique of social institutions without falling into a form of transcendentalism of power and domination. He lacked a conceptually equipped explanation that would allow a differentiation between subjection to power and necessary processes of socialization. This is corroborated by Said who, inspired by Dews, adds:

[Foucault] perceives clearly that institutions are not mere imposed constructs, yet has no apparatus for dealing with this fact, which entails that following a convention is not always equivalent to submitting to a power . . . But without this distinction every delimitation becomes an exclusion, and every exclusion becomes equated with an exercise of power (1994, p. 151).

That Foucault did not explicitly pose ultimate foundations as goals in historical or social transformation, and fought any moral or ethical standard imposed by knowledge or discourses, does not mean that he successfully saved himself from falling into the same trap of posing a determinist and transcendental element in his theory. Such aspect of his theory is reflected in pivotal notions of his work as it will be discussed in the following chapter. Having laid off here some of the basic notions that support Foucault's theory, a conceptual ground has been outlined to deepen its discussion in the light of Castoriadis' framework. Interesting mutual theoretical questions can be now identified after going through a revision of their conceptual apparatus that, far from being exhaustive, allows a comparative discussion between the two authors. Furthermore, many differences have been generally identified as a source of reflection and analysis for the following chapter.

Chapter 5

Society Over the Subject

The main concerns that guided Foucault's work were introduced in the previous chapter. It addressed some fundamental issues in his philosophy such as power and its implication in historical discontinuity and transformation. Determinist and functionalist elements were approached in his framework, and commonalities and divergences with Castoriadis in this respect were posed. The different importance that each author gave to power mediation when elaborating on social institutions was contrasted, and a discussion about the consistency and critical character of their theories was introduced.

This chapter intends to look deeper into the parallel between Castoriadis and Foucault, focusing on the three specific problems of my analysis—the subject, the production of social meaning and representation, and social and cultural change. In so doing, I will evaluate implications of Foucault and Castoriadis' positions regarding freedom and agency; the possibility of reconstructing ourselves and our own subjective/subjectivity constitution; and the critical potential of our individual and collective questioning to transform society. When Foucault's position in relation to these problems is studied from the Castoriadian perspective, it is possible to identify important theoretical issues that affect the political consistency of Foucault's work. Here I argue for Castoriadis' ideas as an alternative to the unresolved problems within Foucault's developments on society, the subject, and social change; problems that Castoriadis saw as foreclosed Foucauldian positions embedded in political relativism.

Foucault on the Subject

Foucault never accepted the subject as a pillar of his theory. Despite the slight theoretical turn Foucault made in his later writings in relation to subjectification, he refused until the end to be committed to a general ontology of the human subject. He assigned neither origin nor essence to the subject, nor gave the subject priority over discourse. Fraser (1989, p. 56) summed up this point, stating that for Foucault the subject constituted only a derivative product of contingent and historical sets of linguistically infused social practices that inscribed power relations upon bodies.

Foucault's project consisted in identifying the way in which what was called the subject was formed, reformed, dispersed, and regulated in discursive reality. Using archaeology he considered how the structure of knowledge delimited the subject, and using genealogy he studied the way in which the body of the subject became the site of the inscription of knowledge and control.

Early, in *The Order of Things* Foucault openly declared, together with structuralists, the death of the subject. In describing the emergence of human sciences, he explicated simultaneously how "man" came to life as a discursive construct. For Foucault, what is called "man" emerged as an object of analysis, of scientific investigation, and as a finite and historically determined being to be studied. This led him to conclude the demise of man as an epistemological subject, backed by the then-emerging French posthumanism, in which the subject was interpreted as an effect of language, desire, and the unconscious. As mentioned in Chapter 4, initially for Foucault, anthropology and psychoanalysis were used to demonstrate how the self-governing cogito or transcendental ground of man would no longer be valid in social analysis.

Psychoanalysis and ethnology are not so much two human sciences among others, but they span the entire domain of those sciences in that they animate its whole surface, spread their concepts throughout it, and are able to propound their methods of decipherment and interpretations everywhere . . . Not only are [psychoanalysis and ethnology] able to do without the concept of man, they are also unable to pass through it, for they always address themselves to that which constitutes his outer limits. One may say of both of them what Lévi-Strauss said of ethnology: that they dissolve man. (Foucault, 1970, p. 379)

Whitebook correctly notes how Foucault's initial acknowledgment of psychoanalysis also had to do with his ambition to pursue a dialogue with unreason, a theoretical and practical program he identified in *Madness and Civilization*[1]. Initially Foucault saw in Freud a potential source to contribute to his objective, though he later turned away from engagement with the inner world of the psyche.

Foucault's refined conception of the subject as a discursive product never implied nor accepted a nonlinguistic psychical dimension such as Freud's notion of the unconscious. However, as Whitebook (2005, p. 315) argued, he struggled with this problem until the end, leaving the extralinguistic dimension of the subject under theorized.[2] For Foucault, the constitution of the subject always depended on the linguistic relationships (discursive and nondiscursive relations). The subject could only be explained as a linguistically mediated result, an external construct infused all the way through by society.

This Foucauldian conception of the subject has been extensively analyzed by different authors and has many different aspects. The point that should be emphasized is that in contrast to Castoriadis, Foucault refused to recognize and theoretically articulate the nonlinguistic dimension of the subject, and instead set theoretical conditions that had problematic consequences for addressing the question of subjectification and change. Castoriadis' reformulation of the Freudian unconscious allowed him to articulate an understanding of psychical representation and subjective configuration.

In his account of unconscious manifestation in the oneiric world, Freud presented an explanation about the nonlinguistic dimension of the subject's psyche. The oneiric world followed its own logic that differed from the waking conscious life and that which did not follow linguistic, logic, or rational principles. Though Freud states that dreams can be made intelligible through reason, he classifies them as products of irrationality. What is at stake in the Freudian account is not only a particular understanding of the subject that incorporates the dialogue of reason and unreason in relation to identity, but also a conceptual platform upon which a new understanding of madness, pathology, and normality can be derived—all primary interests in Foucault's work.

While dreams were never a central topic for Foucault, Freud's approach to dreams involved issues that Foucault explored when he wrote the introduction to Ludwig Binswanger's *Dream and Existence*. In Whitebook's view, in this early text, Foucault had a surrealist and formalist perspective in which the oneiric world is idealized and represents a privileged epistemic position, given that it has no rational censorship.[3] Foucault valorized the dream as a specific form of transcendent imaginary experience with its private and individual character that cannot be exhausted by psychological analysis (1993, p. 43). Foucault stated (1993, p. 35) that within their linguistic structure—which gives life to dreams—the genesis of dreams reflects the original free mode of being of the individual that constitutes it, and offers new possibilities for the individual. Dreams are a result of the mind's capacity to freely generate new images that are not derived from the real—including the memory—that Foucault called imagination.

Imagination referred to the mind's spontaneous image-creating capacity. The imagination is iconoclastic, which means it destroys and consumes all merely given images—including the fundamental representations of the tribe and of the self—projecting a transcendent reality beyond them. Foucault added that the image constituted a ruse of consciousness in order to put a stop to imagining, what he called the moment of discouragement in the hard labor of imagining. To be authentic meant exercising your imagination to transcend the givens of your situation and assume your destiny. The aim of psychotherapy, accordingly, should be to free the imaginary that is trapped in the image—to free the alienation of the imagination (1993, pp. 71–2).

In later writings Foucault abandoned a systematic development of direct questions that emerged from this early work. Specifically, he never took on the concept of imagination with all its conceptual consequences, possibly because of the conflict he entered into with psychoanalysis and the social sciences, as Whitebook (2005) has suggested. These theoretical problems remained tacitly present in his work.

These early observations made by Foucault can be compared to Castoriadis' position in this regard. Commonalities can be identified, as when Foucault, addressing the transgressive dimension of dreams, had a celebratory view about the faculties of imagination that were capable of freely posing creative and self-governing life alternatives to individuals. To a certain extent in the introduction to Ludwig Binswanger's *Dream and Existence,* Foucault's thoughts resembled Castoriadis' discussion of imagination. Both authors agree that the individual's psyche is capable of forming representations in a quid pro quo mode through imagination, of representing and projecting beyond present reality, posing new options and ways of being. Through imagination the subject can de-realize the real, represent its own world, and expand it to the collective dimension.

This concurrence allows us to observe four related questions in which Foucault and Castoriadis greatly differed as their work developed. These differences can be inferred from the theoretical aspects that we have examined: 1) the framework within which they interpret the faculty of psychical representation, or the concept of imagination—called as such in Foucault's early work—the status they give to it, and the role it plays in their respective understandings of representation; 2) the extent to which the products of imagination can be evaluated as new creations or mere reproductions; 3) the way the notion of imagination serves the critical character of each author's theory; and finally, 4) returning to the central issue of this section, the way these questions affect the notion of the subject.

As explained in Chapter 2, Castoriadis sees valuable elements in Freud's *Interpretation of Dreams* to support his ontological notion of imagination, invested with the capacity to create new and not totally determined representations. Foucault, on the contrary, did not engage in a more profound theorization of imagination nor perceive it as a key element in his understanding of representation. As Whitebook points out, the difficulty with Foucault's position in relation to representation is that it is merely descriptive and not worked out thoroughly.[4] In effect, Foucault did not consider the faculty of psychical representation as a necessary problem to be developed.

Castoriadis derives a completely different understanding of representation and the creation of meaning, the subject's socialization into social meaning, and its consequences for individual and social transformation. As seen, Castoriadis seeks a psychoanalytically inspired explanation of representation coherent with a process of subjectification where the infant's psyche goes through progressive stages to become a social entity. In doing so, he assigns a self-agency to the subject that is carefully articulated with other strata or regions of being. In terms of the subjectification or socialization processes, Foucault was interested basically in the effects of power. As Visker (1995, pp. 98–9) suggests, theorizing other processes lacked sense for him. For Foucault, subjectification was reduced to the incorporation of certain forms of power that the individual learned to reproduce. Upon entering society, the subject became a prisoner of that social order in which it learned to function. Foucault highlighted the subject formation process as the assimilation of the individual into society without the infusion of any preexisting privatistic form. Foucault stated:

> The individual is not to be conceived as a sort of elementary nucleus, a primitive atom, a multiple and inert material on which power comes to fasten or against which it happens to strike, and in so doing subdues or crushes individuals. In fact, it is already one of the prime effects of power that certain bodies, certain gestures, certain discourses, and certain desires, come to be identified and constituted as individuals (1980, p. 98).

In the subjectification process Foucault found forms of subjection through which the subject inscribed within itself normalizing principles and made the body a transmogrifying site of disciplinary power. The space of interiority of the subject was carved out of subjectivity by power rather than existing as a deep source of the subject's unconscious. There was no opposition between the interior and the exterior, not because the interior was merely an empty space, but rather because interiority was nothing other than the interiorizing of the outside. As Williams (2001, p. 181) states, this is how Foucault politicized the construction of the subject: all that is outside of the subject forms a hinge for interiority.

Throughout Foucault's work, subjects were products of normalizing practices that eliminated their "psychological irregularities," making docile individuals (1979, p. 170). Through the panoptic effect, Foucault showed how the subject regulated his or her behavior automatically:

> He who is subjected to a field of visibility and who knows it, assumes a responsibility for the constraints of power, he makes them play spontaneously upon himself: he inscribes in himself the power relation in which he simultaneously plays both roles. He becomes the principle of his own subjection (*ibid.*, p. 205).

Foucault described panoptic power as a technique of overlapping subjectification and objectification, as "the subjection of those who are perceived as objects and the objectification of those who are subjected" (*ibid.*, pp. 184–5). In this sense, subjectification became equated to subjection. Foucault wrote: "The man whom we are invited to free, is already in himself the effect of a subjection much more profound than himself" (*ibid.*, p. 30).

Each human individual was seen as an embodied nexus to be transformed by the deployment of external causal powers. The subjectification process was reduced to the range of subject-positions that the discursive realm allowed. But the subject was never considered able to assume an autonomous position as an auto-reflexive entity from whose self, emerged rules of behavior or powerful laws. As seen, he claimed that even a perfectly realized autonomous subjectivity would be a normalized form and a product of disciplinary domination.

Dews (1987) shares this understanding and opinion about Foucault's conception of the subject. In Dews' view, Foucault was immersed in the desire to dissolve the philosophical links between consciousness, self-reflection, and freedom. By establishing a direct relation between subjectification and subjection, Foucault denied that there remained any progressive political potential in the ideal of an autonomous individual. For Foucault any theory of self-determination had to be abandoned, because the free subject was intrinsically heteronomous. And though it could be argued that Foucault in his late works was more interested in the subject's own capacity for constitution or re-constitution within a freer position, there was no room for the concept of self-agency. With self-consciousness abolished, with it went the possibility of a self-ruling subject. Therefore, the aim of political action could not be to enhance or expand any supposed autonomy.

The lack of a drive theory and a psychoanalytical dimension in his work, or even of a phenomenology of the psyche, made Foucault unable to incorporate into his theory an individual site for the production of subjectivity that was capable not only of receiving external contents, but also of elaborating them and even creating new and alternative ones. It was enough to state that the site of production and reproduction of subjectivity (the site of power itself) was a moving substrate of the relationships of forces, where the subject was both a passive recipient and a potential resistance. Even though Foucault considered the emergence of new subjectivities through these resistance processes, this form of subjectivity was difficult to follow since it was not completely theoretically elaborated. Williams (2001) is right to state that what Foucault called "something in the social body which in some senses escapes the relationships of power, a centrifugal movement, an inverse energy to power" (1980, p. 138) remained inadequately theorized, since its origin and character is not explained and its theoretical context (Foucauldian theory itself) left no room to infer it (Williams, 2001, p. 183).

By not providing a theoretical account of: 1) the subject previous to the socialization process; 2) the psychical configuration of the subject as a new being confronting society; and 3) the implied intersubjective process suffered by all subjects in socialization, Foucault was left with no means to explain the psychical process undergone by the subject in the creation and re-creation of subjectivity. Furthermore, Foucault's lack of a psychoanalytical perspective also made him unable to distinguish between the interior and exterior subjective contents, or to understand the processes through which subjects interiorized external contents and built a new subjectivity or became something different from what their society had given them. The differentiated individual and social poles of the psyche elaborated by Castoriadis did not exist in the Foucauldian view.

In relation to the problem of intersubjectivity, Foucault left more theoretical voids or, as Dews (1987, pp. 198–9) has called them, incoherencies. In Dews' view, Foucault's contention that subjects could be forged through objectification—through a nonreciprocal power operation—did not take into account the complexity of intersubjective processes. It was above all incoherent because the human being can only acquire the competencies that transform them into speaking and acting subjects through interaction with other subjects. Foucault's account of a unidirectional surveillance failed to register the fact that socialization depended upon a mutual recognition of subjects. Moreover, the reciprocity that Foucault did evoke was not a kind of reciprocity of communication between equal subjects, but a reciprocity of force that remained embedded within a hierarchy. Thus, although the concept of reciprocity did play an implicitly critical role in Foucault's work, it was not a noncoercive reciprocity that could be made the goal of political struggle. Foucault saw intersubjective relations as totally determined, rendering the subject unable to rework them. In the political arena, intersubjectivity was not a possible space where equal and democratic relations could be established, nor a medium for building more self-governing societies. On the contrary, his view on intersubjective relations had to do only with oppression and inequality; it left no room for a political alternative.

Foucault's notion of the subject hampers a consistent political understanding of society and social change. Especially his notion of resistance -as will be discussed later- prevents him from formulating a more coherent political alternative to envision a better way of life.

Nevertheless, it is undeniable that, up to a point, Foucault theorized a possible transformation of power regimes through the promotion of new forms of subjectivity. However, the way the subject could achieve this was never fully explained. In this regard, Williams (2001, p. 154) noted a paradox that did not favor a satisfactory political resolution in Foucault's work. While the subject was enunciated as the privileged site of political struggle, it was at the same time radically displaced and erased. Likewise, Han (2002, p. 127) saw a conflictual tension between two interpretations of subjectification in Foucault. On the one hand Foucault sees in the subject both: the source of problematization of who he or she is, and the source to transform itself. On the other hand, contradicting the previous statements, Foucault theorizes the subject as inserted into a set of relationships that subject him to power, entirely defining the conditions of possibility for self-constitution. This makes it difficult to say if for Foucault, the subject is a constituting or constituted agent.

Without denying the politicized and critical aspect of Foucauldian theory, or its valuable efforts to break with idealism or metaphysics, the disappearance of the subject in Foucault's theory caused problems for his interest in the subject's freedom, an interest more clearly stated in his later writings. In this respect, Castoriadis' view is more fruitful given that he sees the subject as a fundamental element for collective and self-enfranchisement through social change and autonomy.

Representation and Social Meaning in Foucault

Foucault's concept of meaning stressed the socially constructed nature of reality. Throughout his work, he maintained the poststructuralist principle that meaning was a relative and historical eventuality serving institutionalized social orders. As seen in Chapter 4, social meaning was closely related to his concepts of episteme, discourse, knowledge and power regimes, and social practices. Meanings emerged through different constructions and uses of discourses and were assigned to deeds, facts, and objects by the dominant discourse used by a linguistic community. Moreover, Foucault used the notion of discourse to illustrate the mode of constructing and naming the object of knowledge, which also produced subjectivities and signification.

As already seen, discourse was both the mode of constructing specific-domains or epistemes, and the means of containing the relationships between language and the objects which constituted knowledge. The epistemic ruptures that gave way to new discursive formations, constituted the foundation of his conception about discursively created realities. Foucault's elaboration of meaning was based on the idea that discourse (irreducible to speech) not only worked upon the real, but constructed it.

Foucault contradicted the structuralist perspective when in *The Archaeology of Knowledge* he clearly defended the idea that the rules of formation of discourses were not universal and immutable, nor were they grounded in the mind. They were specific to different discursive domains throughout history. Nevertheless, as Best and Kellner (1991, p. 41) have observed, in a way such rules can be seen as an a priori of all knowledge that constituted the shaping of the perception of truth at different historical moments. These rules were the fundamental codes that constructed an episteme and determined the empirical orders of a particular historical era. They were always at work and also defined practices and morals. In other words, beneath all the related matrices of practices there was the logic of those rules by which meaning was generated.

Power was also deeply involved with representation and the generation of social meaning. In a society, discourse entailed power because the rules determining discourse, enforced norms of what was understood as rational or sane. All discourses were produced by power and through social practices; they were disseminated through various dimensions of social life, corroborating its specific and social-historical meanings.

Foucault's understanding of the social-historical character of meaning and representation resulted in a totally relativistic position toward reality and in general toward different social orders. For Foucault, that there was no such thing as a reality that was not constituted by epistemic or discursive formation implied the relativistic nature of meaning and the possible realities that could originate from it. The diverse and heterogeneous scenarios within which reality could be played out had in essence the same nature and value. Their emergence and configuration came from the same source and worked within the same dynamic. In this sense, Foucault did not worry about the moral ranking of social orders or the adequate or distorted character of cultural representation. His interest was focused on practices and discourse creations where the epistemological dimension was subsumed in relativism when it came to judging right or wrong.

This viewpoint was coherent with his political position toward any normative criterion as a lens for observing, evaluating, or contesting any social order. Since any transformation or modification to a certain power regime meant the rise of a new power structure full of marginalizing social relationships and different forms of subjection, any political compromise with specific political goals or moral maxims meant the discrimination against social sectors and individuals and required the normalization of individuals. In this sense, Foucault did not give any consideration to the judgment of practices supported by complexes of social significations. As a social-historical product representing certain interests, social meaning should be viewed and examined—in Foucault's opinion—without having any moral judgment over them.

Furthermore, specific aspects of the collective and individual dimensions of self-agency in meaning generation also remained insufficiently theorized. The social-historical field for Foucault was defined as something imposed rather than a freely created realm for self-constitution. The source of discourses was diluted through the whole society, and the particular means of their creation never constituted a major concern for Foucault. The questions: "What enabled humans to create meaning?" "What differentiated humans as social beings?" and, "how were humans able to produce meaning and represent their reality?" were never explicitly posed or answered by Foucault, despite the fact that all these questions were at the heart of his work and contributions.

Foucault's concepts of discourse, episteme, social practices, and so forth, implied that the meaning and signification that gave them life and encompassed them were already present in society. The source of meaning was taken as a given. Within his framework, representing and assigning meaning to reality was never analyzed deeply enough by Foucault.

The assertion made by Dreyfus and Rabinow (1983, p. xix) in this respect did not shed light onto this question. Stating—as they did—that Foucault's goal was to renounce to any attempt to understand a meaning-giving subject in a phenomenological sense still presupposed an explanation of representation in Foucault that in my view was not refined or satisfactory. As meaning is intrinsic to representation, it became evident that Foucault also left a void here. He did not discuss extensively enough how individuals alone, and in society, generated and experienced their own subjective reality. The principle by which he defended the possible existence of the multiplicity of realities (discourses, knowledge, and power regimes) throughout history presupposed a capacity in humans to represent or imagine their own world-views. In this sense, psychical representation was at the heart of his theory, but Foucault never theorized it in an exhaustive way.

By contrast, Castoriadis elaborates a theory of representation through which he defines the main difference between humans and the rest of living beings. It is through the afunctional representation of the human psyche that human beings generate a rupture with fixed instinctual regulations. This is the capacity of the psyche to create an image out of external stimuli on the body free of restriction by canonic patterns that only obey biological needs and seek their satisfaction. A direct consequence of this singular capacity—unique to humans—is the predominance of representational pleasure over organ pleasure, evidenced in the separation of sexuality and reproduction. This explains why it is only humans who obtain pleasure out of sexual fetishism, for example.

Castoriadis' explanation of psychical representation allows him to explain the existing relationship between the biological and the psychical domains of human beings without falling into a dualism of soma and psyche. Castoriadis relies on Freudian drive theory, in which biological instinctual drives can only be manifested in the psyche by means of representation. Quoting Freud, Castoriadis affirms that the psyche "submits the drives to the obligation of a delegation through representation" (1987, p. 282). To Castoriadis this means that instinctual drives and the afunctionalized imagination cannot be thought separately. The leaning-on, or anaclisis, explanation allows him to establish a relationship between the biological and the social that cannot be conceived as an evolutionary consequence. Body and mind are not antinomies but are connected through different strata or regions of being.

I disagree with Klooger (2009, p. 85) when he stated that by taking up the Freudian leaning-on explanation or anaclisis, parts of Castoriadis' own writings betray the need to reformulate the Western philosophical dichotomy between psyche and body.[5] On the contrary, I find a great potential in Castoriadis' argumentation to question Western philosophical dualistic traditions, precisely because of the way he reformulates this Freudian insight. It is important to recall that Freud introduced the notion of anaclisis[6] to explain the relationship between the sexual drives and the self-preservative functions as the former initially leaning on the latter. Though the sexual drives are part of the somatic domain they become independent and are not reducible to it. Drives are the "ambassadors" to the psyche and are consubstantial to psychical representation. Castoriadis' advance in relation to Freud's elaboration on representation is to overcome Freudian determinism by proposing the concept of radical imagination that enables an undetermined representation in the psyche.

For Castoriadis the body and the psyche cannot be conceived separately. The body is understood within his theory of representation. Castoriadis conceptualizes the body as an imaginary creation that leans on its physical and biological substrate without being completely determined by it. The body is already a representation that incarnates SIS through sublimation and socialization though, in contrast to Foucault, it is not exhausted by them. Despite the fact that both authors agree that, through representation in the form of social canons, the body, its needs, pleasures, and satisfactions are constructed, defined, and given meaning, only Castoriadis builds a theory of representation that takes into account the body as a biological entity. Foucault's theory, on the contrary, obliterates the biological dimension of the body.

As seen in Chapter 4, through his genealogical perspective Foucault focused on the body and its relationship with representation and subjectivity. Progressively he centered on sexuality as a fertile realm in which to analyze this triad and the effects of power. He formulated structural concepts such as bio-power and wrote about bodies and pleasures, however, he did not explore the biological aspects attached to sexuality, nor was there any scientific attempt to theorize it. Whitebook (2005, pp. 334–7) illustrated this well, showing how far Foucault's constructivism went when he argued that a biological substratum of sexuality is virtually an illusion. Because he wanted to avoid the dangers of naturalism and essentialism, the somatic dimension of sexuality, bodies, and pleasures remained unexplored. Sexuality for Foucault was completely constructed and came from the outside as a product of power. Bodies and pleasures could be shaped and reshaped through control and domination without evident biological constraints. This was congruent with Foucault's main goal of making evident the ties existing between the body, representation, and subjectivity without making any room for scientific or normalizing discourses, as he called psychoanalysis.

Here once again the different approach to psychoanalysis made by Foucault and Castoriadis are revealing. Foucault's rejection of psychoanalysis results in a narrow and limited explanation about the biological dimension of the human body, and its existing relation to representation and subjectivity. As seen, Foucault was reluctant to admit the theoretical need to explain the biological component present in every human representation, in this case the human body and its desires. On the contrary, Castoriadis uses and reinterprets Freudian teachings about the body's instinctual drives, admitting the biological and natural dimension of the human body. Like Foucault, Castoriadis defines the body as a representation, as a social construction. However, as explained in this section, Castoriadis gives an important place to the biological dimension of the body and provides his own original explanation about its relation to the psychical representation and its subjective contents. In other words, contrary to Foucault, Castoriadis has a theoretical explanation of psychical representation where the natural and biological reality of the human body is acknowledged and taken into account. This demonstrates how Foucault's and Castoriadis' different takes on psychoanalysis favored a better articulated explanation about the subject, meaning, and representation in Castoriadis, while in Foucault it left unanswered questions and theoretical limitations.

Why Should We Change?

Social change and politics were controversial issues for Foucault. His intention was to deny a theory of modernist emancipation and to build a critique of social-historical formations, explaining their relative character and authoritative effects on individuals and society. The question is whether his theory is critical or not, and if so, to what extent it can be stated that his proposal is a consistent and all-encompassing theory that make possible critical politics.

Foucault has been regarded as a critical icon in the social sciences and philosophy during the last decades. Rightly, the literature has stressed the original and primarily critical intention of Foucault's work. Common interpretations note how Foucault questioned what was conceived as critical and revolutionary thinking at his time and reevaluated the role of intellectuals. The constant inquiry and the reflective attitude about historically situated practices he called for have been interpreted as echoing legacies of major thinkers such as Kant (Rabinow, 1994) or Nietzsche (Sluga, 2005). Likewise, the political character of his theory has been analyzed for its undeniable ethical dimension (Davidson, 2005; Bernauer and Mahon, 2005).

Authors, such as Rajchman (1985, pp. 34–8, 93–123), sum up well, the common arguments in regard to Foucault's politics. In their view, Foucault proposed a new ethic of constant disengagement from constituted forms of experience in order to free oneself for the invention of new forms of life. In defending a historical nominalism, Foucault introduced new understandings of political struggle, without appealing to absolutes or notions such as "pure consciousness" to end domination. Freedom lay in the capacity to find alternatives to particular forms of discourse and being. But what is most important to note here, because it constitutes a major difference with Castoriadis, is that Foucault's core politics of subjectivity found its roots in an analysis of the historical forms of the constitution of the subject without proposing any principle or condition to differentiate among them. This is contrary to what Castoriadis does, who by proposing his concept of autonomy provides us with a referent to differentiate and value subjective contents and social-historical forms.

In short, Foucault's urgency to replace the idealist notion of final emancipation results in a nominalist concept of endless revolt that constitutes the backbone of Foucault's politics and the critical character of his theory.

Analyzed from the perspective of Castoriadis' philosophy, Foucault's critical position reveals and confirms theoretical voids that limit its potentiality and undermine the idea of social change. One of Foucault's critical pillars, his concept of resistance, constitutes a starting point for this debate. The reach of this notion, which presupposed contesting and modifying power regimes and social orders, is well illustrated by what Foucault called *counter-discourses*. Counter-discourses materialized and expressed ways of resistance through their potential to subvert normalized subject identities, forms of consciousness, objects of knowledge, and forms of desire and pleasure. However, despite promoting critical reflection and having a transgressive potential, there was no explanation of why they were different from previously instituted discourses or biopolitics. Fraser (1989, pp. 55–66) has demonstrated this point in Foucault's work by analyzing his elaborations on bodies and forms of pleasures. She correctly noted that there was no explanation of how bodies and pleasures emerged from resistance and counter-discourses that were different from previous forms of sexuality experienced in normalizing strategies and institutions.

Foucault's treatment of power made it difficult to establish differentiated forms of subjection, and thereby establish better or worse social practices or relations. Having defined power as an all-encompassing and strategic constituent that mediated all social relations and structured societies, it became difficult to differentiate among socio-historical formations. Power had no specific grounding and, as a corollary, resistance had no specific locus either. Foucault's concept of power was too general, making difficult to see against what power operated. Did it operate against a possible freer subject? Or, would there be any substantial difference in case power was cancelled? Certainly, Foucault had negative answers to these questions. In his theory, power acquired an almost metaphysical status, always being produced and reproduced. Even though he stated that wherever there was power there was resistance, his theoretical model did not encourage resistance. There was no possible political agenda against power or its abuse. As Sarup (1993, pp. 81–3) reiterated, Foucault refused to answer the questions of what should be resisted, on what basis, and what would we expect to accomplish with acts of resistance. Nussbaum (1999, p. 3) echoes this observation, adding that in Foucault all individuals are prisoners of an all-enveloping structure of power, and any reform movement ends up serving power in new, insidious ways.

As mentioned in Chapter 4, this Foucauldian stance was a derivative consequence of his position in relation to normative criteria. As Fraser (1989, pp. 19–21, 27) stated, Foucault pretended to give an account that was both politically engaged and normatively neutral, affirming that his work lacked any parameter upon which a differentiated judgment could be made. This is due to the fact that he refrained from offering a normative justification and validity to different power and knowledge regimes. Though Foucault distinguished between forms of domination and social formations in history—for example, his explicit preference for specific values such as those of the ancient Greek aesthetic of existence—he did not set the normative standard that his theory needed in order to establish a criterion to differentiate among them. From the statement that there could not be power-free societies, social practices, and knowledge, it does not follow that all forms of power are normatively equivalent, or that one could not object to a form of life simply on the ground that it was power-laden. But in any case, if it is accepted that power is everywhere, then, we need to differentiate among possible kinds of power(s) and the way power(s) is inflicted or exercised. Whitebook underlines this aspect by stating:

> [B]ecause he suspects that all forms of *normativity* are masked forms of *normalization*, Foucault cannot and will not address the question of how to evaluate them. Given, therefore, that the effects of power are

intentionally generated for purposes of social engineering and that they cannot in any sense claim to be positive, I don't see how the thesis of the productivity of power provides an answer to Foucault's critics [in relation to his totalizing view of power] (Whitebook, n.d.)

Only with the introduction of normative notions could Foucault have answered inherent questions in his work, such as: why struggle and resistance were better than submission and how they differed (Fraser, 1989, pp. 29–32).

The normative dimension of Castoriadis' work constitutes a major difference from Foucault. While the former is able to introduce this dimension in order to justify and give value to social change, the latter avoided it for fear of falling into a narrative of progressive humanism or a historical teleology marked by idealist, humanist, or rationalist principles.

Authors like Simons (1995, pp. 60–7, 114) have justified the absence of a normative dimension in Foucault's work. He states that introducing a normative dimension in Foucault's theory would have presupposed using humanist principles that appealed to universalisms. Castoriadis contradicts this assumption demonstrating that normative differentiation between social orders, SIS, institutions, power regimes or epistemes, does not necessarily entail universalist principles.

As I have shown, the nature and characteristics of the principle of autonomy in Castoriadis allow us to pose the normative question in a different terrain that does not imply transcendental figures, ethnocentric universalisms, or other modernist traps that both authors sought to challenge. Clearly, both Foucault and Castoriadis share common elements in their interpretation of social change. In their politics of subjectivity, both authors emphasize auto-reflectiveness, permanent questioning, and social forms that promote new practices and conceptions of being. Both think that despite the constant presence of power, practicing liberty may enable new social forms. Furthermore, they coincide on the fluid nature of power that cannot be reified or allocated in specific relationships or sole institutions. However, Foucault's determinism relating to power becomes especially evident when addressing social change, given that he forecloses any possibility to theorize a creative dimension in individuals or society that could not only reproduce power but create something new. Meanwhile, Castoriadis fights determinism in order to eloquently articulate the political dimension of his theory. He also brings forward a normative dimension that is theoretically coherent with his position, establishing another major difference between him and Foucault. A crucial element that separates them is their disagreement regarding setting parameters and standards that would allow judgment and put forward a new understanding of difference, as does Castoriadis. In my view, these two points make Castoriadis' critical perspective a better-articulated and consistent option with which to evoke action and substantiate social change. As Bernstein (1984, pp. 225–31) has corroborated, Foucault left us with an unfinished and not fully thematized ethical-political perspective, where preferences for desirable social forms and changes are empty and vacuous, given that we do not know which possibilities and changes are desirable or why. Walzer (1983) also sees voids in Foucault's theoretical and political positioning. He sees it as a childish outrunning of a consistent argumentation that should support any political struggle. Referring to Foucault, Walzer states:

> One can't be downcast, angry, indignant . . . embittered *with reason* unless one inhabits some social setting and adopts, however tentatively and critically, its codes and categories. Or unless, and this is much harder, one constructs a new setting and proposes new codes and categories. Foucault refuses to do either of these things, and that refusal, which makes his genealogies so powerful and so relentless, is also the catastrophic weakness of his political theory (Walzer, 1983, p. 490).

As discussed throughout this book, to the question: "why should we change?", neither Foucault nor Castoriadis has an answer based on transcendental criteria or ultimate standards emanating from absolute sources or authorities. Neither of them would respond with arguments that they would say came from extrasocial sources. However, they do not coincide in their political projects. Foucault encourages pursuing local resistance by strategizing against any power expression. In the case of social theory that means unmasking the microphysics of power and its embodiment in material objects, human bodies, and normalized daily practices. As valuable as it might be, it is equally limited not only because of the way it is conceptualized but also because its short-sighted horizon of action. Castoriadis' project of autonomy is articulated and rooted in his definition of radical democracy. Change directed to what he envisions as autonomous subjects and collectives, entails social institutions that allow effective and direct political participation where democratic self-regulation and self-limitation is practiced. That, he argues, is very different from the political apparatuses, monopolies, and institutions that run and structure today's democratic or semidemocratic systems. Putting them into question as a tension between heteronomy and autonomy is consubstantial with democratic transformations.

Chapter 6

Castoriadis versus Foucault: Concluding Remarks

Sharing the same social and historical context, Foucault and Castoriadis present us with two diverging interpretations of their common conditions of theoretical production. They envisioned new angles from which to approach social practices and institutions within their substantially distinct frameworks, each of them with its own limitations and contributions.

The critique of power and its mode of being at different moments in history was Foucault's main contribution. Justifiably, his understanding of power, its capillary nature and the insidious ways in which it operates, gained him wide recognition as the theorist of power par excellence. In a brilliant intellectual exercise, Foucault was able to illustrate the deployment of poststructuralist principles in central social institutions. Using powerful rhetorical accounts of what he called the "discredited" and "marginalized" in history, he demonstrated the potential meaning of what is hidden or overlooked in society, an insight that was reflected in multiple new research agendas. The categories he built to study the techniques of power and its domination effects, from the human body and forms of pleasure to forms of governmentality are potent and allow meticulous analysis of quotidian practices that became naturalized and normalized. Reasonably, social scientists have extensively used his conceptual apparatus and methods as a "toolkit"—as was Foucault's intention—in their anthropological, sociological, philosophical, and historical studies.

On the other hand, Castoriadis' major contribution is his ontology of creation and the project of autonomy. His critique of determinism present in the Western ontological tradition makes his work unique and original. It also provides a renewed sense of critical thinking, where agency and self-determination are at the core of his notion of politics and radical democracy.

By comparing central notions in both frameworks, this book has illustrated how Foucault and Castoriadis substantiated their work based on conflicting epistemological perspectives and distinct concepts of subjectivity, autonomy, agency, power, and social change. In doing so, social and historical determinism has been analyzed as a central characteristic of Foucault's work, contrasting it to Castoriadis' ontology of creation—presented here as a radical alternative to Foucault's more widely accepted thinking.

Foucault departed from epistemological and political relativism, leading to a linguistic idealism that denied the world any external reality independent of language or discourse, and that denied the subject any agency in the creation of social reality. Going in a different direction, Castoriadis sought to develop a more critical theory with an ontological background. He postulated an explanation of the totality of the existing-being, in which different strata of being interacted to create the social world of the subject, where the subject could be recuperated as the author of his or her own reality. This ontology of creation makes a strong counterbalance to Foucauldian perspectivism while still opposing total epistemological objectivism.

Most significantly, Foucault's and Castoriadis' distinct takes on subjectivity and agency reflect on the different critical and political potentialities derived from their theories. Foucault's lack of a comprehensive theory of intersubjectivity—that finds its corollary in his famous "death of man"—obliterated the notion of autonomy and undermined the subject's agency. Foucault's notion of agency was exhausted in his idea of a resistance anchored in the deterministic and pervasive character of power that dominated any possible subjective change or historical rupture. Trapped in relativism, the type of social critique or resistance that derives from his work lacks a normative standard by which to define human rights and distinguish among collective choices, social practices, forms of life, and diverse cultural formations.

More productively, Castoriadis develops an ontology that uses a psychoanalytical explanation of the intersubjective processes to not only provide an account of individual subjectivity, but also pose an original notion of agency. Equipped with a nondetermined and creative agency, Castoriadis' subject is able to judge and opt among social institutions and practices where autonomy works as both a normative standard and a political option.

The substantial differences between Foucault and Castoriadis have been studied through an analysis centered on three main notions: the subject, the production of social meaning and representation, and social and cultural change.When approaching Foucault's and Castoriadis' similarities and divergences in relation to the subject, their reception of psychoanalysis has been identified as a major point of difference. Castoriadis' reformulation of Freudian principles allows him to theorize a socially created subject that could become detached from its own personal and social identity to enable self-reflection and creation. Here, his concept of radical imagination is an original contribution in the light of his attempt to break the western philosophical deterministic ontology from Plato to our days.

Foucault rejected any contribution from Freud. After an ambiguous relationship with Freud's work, he concluded that psychoanalysis represented another way of normalizing and controlling individuals. Nevertheless, Foucault's discerning intelligence did not ignore subjectivity as a central question to achieve his theoretical goals. He paid much attention to subjective contents of individuals and the way power modeled them. But he lacked the theoretical tools to satisfactorily explain the intersubjective dimension that individual subjectivity presupposes. In other words, even though subjectivity was central to Foucault, he never explained sufficiently the relational process between individuals and society that shapes, informs, and constitutes their subjectivities. Subjectivity in Foucault is limited to the imposition of external social forms of power. His desire to disintegrate the autonomous rational ego and defend decentered and plural forms of subjectivity took him into a form of transcendentalism where the subject could only be conceived as a product of omnipotent, omnipresent, and, in a way, homogeneous power.

Foucault theorized neither a space nor an instance where individuals could rationally distance and emancipate themselves in an autonomous way from the contents provided by society. Self-reflection was never an instance elaborated theoretically by Foucault to account for its appearance in any decision taken by the subject. Foucault suspected that the promise of the benefits of the exercise of reason had totalitarian implications, and argued in favor of a plurality of "forms of rationality" that would compete and overlap as instruments of domination.

The Castoridian notion of the subject as an undetermined entity with irreducible and indissoluble individual and social poles strongly contrasts with the absent concept of the subject in Foucault. Castoriadis contests this structuralist and poststructuralist view by seeing the subject as a creative self, mediated by social institutions. Using the Freudian notion of the unconscious, Castoriadis reworks the problem of psychical representation in order to explain the creative character of the human being. His concept of radical imagination supports his idea of indetermination manifested and expressed in the social-historical dimension of society, as well as in its ISS and social institutions.

Furthermore, his elaborations on the individual and social poles of the subject throws light on the old problem in the social sciences of whether the subject should be considered an individual agency or a collective product, and the false belief that society is the sum of individual subjectivities. Here, Castoriadis integrates psychoanalytic contributions into an anthropological and sociological account. Using psychoanalysis he explains how the individual constitutes his subjectivity by interiorizing external social contents given by its society to ensure the permanency of the instituted imaginary, but at the same time can re-imagine such contents and redefine them from a self-ruling position.

In this sense, Castoriadis' notion of subjectivity substantially differs from Foucault's. Castoriadis offers an explanation of the stratification of the individual psyche and its subjective contents, and also—contrary to Foucault—posits an individual space for reflection and the possibility for emancipatory transformation at the individual and the social levels.

Castoriadis' and Foucault's differences when theorizing the subject are directly linked to their distinct conceptions of meaning and representation. Their perspectives with regard to these issues are contradictory. Even though they agreed on the social nature and the historical and dynamic character of meaning and, most importantly, neither defended a unique ideal model of society, Castoriadis debates the Foucauldian approach to meaning. Foucault interpreted meaning within a "homogenous pluralism" where multiple social meanings or significations are always a mere reproduction of power effects. On the contrary, Castoriadis establishes standards by which to differentiate among social or cultural significations or meanings.

Castoriadis' theory of psychical representation explains meaning generation and its afunctional and noncanonic character. He is not satisfied with stating that social meaning is imposed on individuals in order to keep society together and functioning, even though his theory explains the functional aspects of meaning and its unifying role within social institutions. Furthermore, he is eager to demonstrate how meaning is undeterminably originated by social individuals and their collectives, an idea that is complemented by his notions of creation and autonomy. While Foucault saw meaning as determined by its power to dominate and control individuals and society, Castoriadis re-elaborates meaning as a social creation that is not totally determinant or determined.

Castoriadis does not believe that because social institutions and their constitutive meanings are historically contingent and socially created, and plural forms of meaning have to be understood without universalizing, it must necessarily be concluded that everything is (means) the same. In other words, accepting these two facts does not justify a naïve relativistic position before, for example, social institutions or culturally diverse practices. Moreover, in acknowledging that the social legitimation of any ISS, institution, or social formation is provided by the society that creates and experiences them, Castoriadis defends a normative standard by which to critically examine social and cultural contents of different societies without accepting or relying on ethnocentrism, evolutionary, or colonialist views.

As emphasized throughout this book, all these moves led Foucault and Castoriadis to very different political positions. The relativistic and deterministic aspects of Foucault's developments ended up in what Castoriadis calls the glorification of eclecticism, conformity, sterility, and banality, and the abandonment of the critical function of thinking (Castoriadis, 1997t, p. 42). As many times criticized here, the deterministic role that Foucault assigned to power ruled out a plausible political alternative that could consider social change free of determinacy.

Even though in Foucault the discursive constructions embedded in subjectivities or knowledge regimes can be resisted, modified, and changed in a moment of openness this possibility does not have sufficient weight in Foucault's elaboration. The limits set to possible transformations of formative elements of discourses illustrate this point. Although there can be changes through what Foucault called counter-discursive practices, the aesthetics of existence, technologies of the self, or forms of desire, the question remains: "what does this change mean or imply?". One thing is clear: change does not imply the emergence of anything unprecedented that does not simply reproduce what was already beneath existing social contents.

Foucault differentiated among historical forms of domination and in his later writings he appealed to a possible subjective reconstruction of individuals to live better forms of life, differentiating in this way between "worse" and "better" ways of living. However, he never substantiated this position. Foucault did not provide an articulated theoretical body that justified a normative standard to value forms of life; to understand how, through processes of subjective transformation, individuals could bring new and freer subjective contents; or to acknowledge social change.

In sum, it is possible to say that when thinking about possibilities of changing or overcoming powerful and controlling social formations, Foucault left theoretical voids, particularly as illustrated in his notion of resistance. Despite the critical potentiality of resistance and the proclaimed productive character of power, it has to be recognized that he framed these notions within a context of determination that left him unable to explain why differences in, for example, new forms of bodies, desires, and/or discourses could be distinguished and why they were essentially different.

This position is also reflected in Foucault's understanding of the social role of theory. As a poststructuralist, he only believed in local resistance and rejected the idea of macropolitics or a radical project of social reconstruction. In his eyes, theory is an instrument in the service of a particular struggle. He warned about the danger of intellectuals being agents that reproduced the system of power they were immersed in, where their ideas of social responsibility or consciousness were shaped by that very system. The only possible role of intellectuals for Foucault was to struggle against the forms of power that imprisoned them by revealing and undermining power where it was most insidious (Foucault, 1977, pp. 205–8).

Foucault defended intellectuals who used their specialized work and expertise to carry out a political struggle against power within their particular social settings. He saw theory as a local practice distanced from a totalizing theoretical project. This constitutes another theoretical and political difference between Foucault and Castoriadis, who, from his early works, defends the idea of a theoretical and political project that, as a product of its social conditions of emergence, worked as an instance to critically reflect upon them and promote autonomous changes.

Castoriadis and Foucault negated the belief that there is a totalizing, complete, and definitive knowledge. However, Castoriadis does not share Foucault's position regarding the role of theory. As Bernstein (1995) rightly pointed out, Castoriadis sees theory as a social practice. He terms the work of clarifying from within history an understanding of what being in history means, elucidation. The activity of elucidation is consonant with the indeterminate nature of history (Bernstein, 1995, p. 203): it does not have a grounding origin or a determinate telos, nor does it seek transparency or mastery. In this sense, Castoriadis distances himself from seeking the modernist totalizing project of knowledge. He contemplates another possibility: acknowledging the undetermined character of the social-historical and the incomplete and endless nature of knowledge and theory still leaves room to recuperate a critical normative political instance understood in terms of autonomy.

Linking the project of autonomy to the practice of theory is consistent with his ontology of creation. As seen, without grounding it in metaphysical modes of thinking, the critical character of Castoriadis' theory resides to a great extent in his project of autonomy. His notions of subject, subjectivity, and subjectification, as well as that of the instituting and instituted power of the social imagination, substantiate the normative character of autonomy and explicate social transformation. As discussed in this text, Castoriadis develops through his whole theoretical work, the notions that Foucault failed to theoretically sustain in his later period. Castoriadis provides a solid notion of the subject equipped with the capacity to reflect, question, deliberate, and create; a consistent theory of psychoanalytically engaged subjectification, that allowed an understanding of the individual and social poles of the subject; a logically articulated social-historical dimension where the instituting and instituted power of society can interact and overcome heteronomy; and a norm or standard of superior validity that allows us to politically discern, debate, and opt our social institutions.

In consequence, the comparison between Foucault and Castoriadis shows why Castoriadis falls neither into deterministic conceptions of society and the human subject nor into relativistic positions. Even though the project of autonomy in Castoriadis can evoke further philosophical and political discussions that are far from being totally conclusive, it goes further and is more productive. Castoriadis articulates in a more consequent and comprehensive way the critical status of theory that goes beyond a fashionable "pomo" academic position.

Castoriadis, without the Foucauldian shortcomings, is able to move forward and link his theoretical and political activity to his vision of a new ontology, where the human being is understood in a completely new manner; and the determined and the undetermined can be conceptualized along with a specific social and political project. It is through elucidation that Castoriadis builds an ontology that theorizes simultaneously the inherently ambiguous, undetermined, and contingent character of a given organization of the world—the magmatic—while also contemplating its determined, precise, and predictable dimension—the identitary/ensemblist.

He presents a theory of closure and openness, permanency and change, heteronomy and autonomy, where a postmetaphysical decentered notion of collective self-institution is at the core of radical democratic politics. Without appealing to an absolute source of ultimate authority that would ground once and for all normative principles, it provides enough normative and standard sources to evaluate social change and value social practices (Kalyvas, 1998a, pp. 176–7).

Distanced from poststructuralism, Castoriadis provides a singular response to the same critiques this intellectual movement made in relation to modernist, rationalistic, objectivist, and positivists views. More interesting is the fact that he renews the notion of critical thinking and radical change within a social context and a historical moment where this goal has been sunk in disillusionment, naïve relativism, conformism, and insignificancy, as Castoriadis puts it.

The ontology of creation, which in Castoriadis' view might bring new political perspectives and more democratic and autonomous social institutions, poses no minor challenge to the way we understand society and the Being. As for Aristotle, for Castoriadis "Being" is Chaos, Abyss, and Groundlessness. It entails the continuously suspended fragility and precariousness of meaning and of our cathected objects, works, affects, and desires: the mortality of the Self (Castoriadis, 1997q, 136). Nonetheless, "Being" is also creation and undetermined imagination, which find their best expression in Art and Politics, as Castoriadis knew it.

Notes

Introduction

[1] Aglietta (1987) and Lipietz (1996) analyze the impact of Fordism and its consequences in terms of consumption patterns and production, as well as on labor relations through managerial schemes and wage regulations. From a distinct point of view, Ross (1999) makes an interesting examination of crucial cultural transformations that took place in France from the mid-1950s to the mid-1960s, showing how those were key elements in shaping the French intellectual and artistic productions in the following decades.

[2] Taylor (1979) discusses in depth Hegelian issues that influenced French debates during this period.

[3] Bourdieu (1993) showed how bodies of knowledge understood as historical and cultural productions are shaped and structured by political affairs, social conjunctures, and networks of legitimized agents in public and academic spheres. Boschetti (1988) followed these premises and illustrated Sartre's case in France.

[4] Macey (1995) and Eribon (1991) agree on this historical account.

Chapter 1

[1] Lefort was a French sociologist and philosopher who worked with Merleau-Ponty and who co-founded SB.

[2] At this time the Communist Party (CP) had some 700 militants in France.

[3] Yugoslavia, as well as Russia's other satellite countries, was considered as a country where the revolution had not been totally successful because the CP had not nationalized everything in the very beginning and because it had kept in place a few ministers who did not formally belong to the CP (Castoriadis, 1997m, p. 4).

[4] All these intellectuals were influenced by different theoretical trends being discussed in France at that moment. In the case of Castoriadis' early writings, besides Marx it is possible to say that Max Weber and Merleau-Ponty had some influence. Adams (2007, pp. 46–7) alludes further to the influence Castoriadis received from Schelling, Fichte and Heidegger, primarily during his SouB period. I am not especially interested in tracking the effects of these thinkers in this chapter. It is more pertinent for my argument to examine how Castoriadis' militancy and his analysis about the socio-political context, led him to reinterpret revolutionary actions and socialism, opening up a new theoretical path that would distance him from Marx and other inherited philosophical traditions. As Honneth (1986, pp. 62–78) argues, it is especially interesting how, at this

stage, Castoriadis prepares the ground for a particular interpretation of the category of praxis that he will connect to a whole theory of society, introducing revolutionary action as the pivotal idea that aims at autonomy.

In his work, Castoriadis acknowledges Merleau-Ponty's contributions. Later on Castoriadis distances himself from Merleau-Ponty. See his texts: "The Sayable and the Unsayable: Homage to Merleau-Ponty" (Castoriadis, 1984b) and "Merleau-Ponty and the Weight of the Ontological Tradition" (Castoriadis, 1993b). Adams (2011) presents an elaborate discussion about Merleau-Ponty and Castoriadis.

[5] The extensive and complex analysis Castoriadis made of Marxism started to be done at SouB but did not conclude there. I do not intend to make an exhaustive review of his entire critique to Marxism here. I will restrict myself to the main Marxist notions that Castoriadis judged as deterministic and which, in his view, deserved to be reconceptualized.

[6] Cohn-Bendit, the important student leader of May' 68, wrote in his book on May 1968 about the debt of the left-wing alternative to Socialisme ou Barbarie saying: 'I am not and do not want to be—anything but a plagiarist when it comes to preaching of revolutionary theory' and 'the views we have been presenting are those of P. Chaulieu.' (Paul Chaulieu was one of Castoriadis' pseudonyms.) (Cohn-Bendit quoted by Curtis, 1988, p. x).

[7] The group established contacts with similar organizations in other countries and helped to found what became "*Solidarity*" in England, which eventually inspired a like-named group in Philadelphia. The West Indian historian C.L.R. James was an important figure to SouB who worked together with Raya Dunayevska, Trotsky's former secretary.

[8] It is clear that any attempt to divide the life and work of SB into periods carries serious problems in reflecting the real developments and dynamic of the group. As noted previously, this artificial division made here has expository purposes. It was made on the basis of a first attempt suggested by Castoriadis (1997m, pp. 1–34). Another attempt at SouB periodization was done by Gottraux (1997). Castoriadis publicly disagreed with its content and questioned its veracity.

[9] 'During this period [1949–53] the immediate public of the group and the review was made up of what was left of the old-style 'ultra left' groups: Bordigists, Council Communists, a few anarchists, and some offspring of the 1920s German "leftists." These groups were breaking up or disappearing at a rather rapid pace' (Castoriadis, 1997m, p. 5).

[10] Lefort and Simon formed a group called Information set Liaisons Ouvriéres (ILO), which later was named Information set Correspondance Ouvriéres (ICO). The position formulated by Lefort was published in *SB* No. 26 and reprinted in 1979 (Lefort, 1979).

[11] The Greek Civil War (December 1944–January 1945 and 1946–9) was a two-stage conflict during which Greek communists unsuccessfully tried to gain control of Greece.

[12] Originally published as "Socialisme ou Barbarie," *SB* No. 1 (March 1949). It was originally translated as "Socialism Reaffirmed" by Bob Pennington and printed as *Solidarity Pamphlet* in 1961. Later reproductions quoted here were published as "Presentation of Socialisme ou Barbarie: An Organ of Critique and

Revolutionary Orientation"(Castoriadis, 1997o, pp. 35–40) and "Socialism or Barbarism"(Castoriadis, 1988i, pp. 76–106).

[13] This was originally published in *SB* No. 1 (March 1949).

[14] Castoriadis started to develop his theory of bureaucratic capitalism in the first six issues of *SB* in the following articles: "Editorial: Socialisme ou Barbarie" (No. 1); "Les Rapports de la Production en Russie" (No. 2); "La Consolidation Temporaire du Capitalisme Mondial" (No. 3); "L'Exploitation de la Paysannerie sous le Capitalisme Bureaucratique" (No. 4); and "La Bureaucratique Yougoslave" (No. 5/6).

[15] This notion appeared in the Castoridian publications as early as 1949. Born out of the major political events in France and abroad, this notion came to life as a logical and consequent resolution of the political diagnosis that Castoriadis and his colleagues had made about contemporary societies. Later on, this notion would become central in his major political and philosophical work. Castoriadis refined it, inspired by political developments as well as by other theoretical influences such as psychoanalysis. The notion of self-management Castoriadis worked with at this point in time could be seen as the roots of his later notion of autonomy; however, the theoretical content it embraced in 1949 is far from what Castoriadis would conceptualize as political collective and individual autonomy.

[16] Castoriadis cites pseudonyms such as Chaze and Vega as members that were in disagreement with the general position of the group.

[17] Later on, Claude Lefort, whose pseudonym was "Montal," would publish his position toward these issues in 1979 in *Eléments d'une Critiqué à la Bureaucratique* (Lefort, 1979).

[18] Molina (1998) quotes Lefort from the texts: *L'Antimythes* ("An interview with Claude Lefort") No.14, 1975, p. 4 and *Eléments d'une Critiqué à la Bureaucratique* (Paris: Gallimard, 1979).

[19] These opinions were expressed in *SB* No.3.

[20] This thesis was sustained by the group since 1949 in their first issue and also in the text "La Consolidation Temporaire du Capitalisme Mondial" (*SB* No.3).

[21] Here Castoriadis makes reference to Marx's interpretation of the process of concentration that would not stop until a single capitalist or group of capitalists predominated.

[22] Raymond Hirzel (Bourt Gaspardd), Albert Maso (Vega), Jacques Signorelli (Garros) and Martine Gautrat. Georges Petit also joined the group in 1951 and by the end of 1952, Henri Simon was a member.

[23] This event refers to the uprising that took place in Berlin during June 1953, especially from the 8–18 when 60% of workers at the "Stalinallee"(an East German construction project started in 1949 in Stalin's honor) rejected the majority of the working norms imposed by the government. This resulted in a strike against the Party and official Unions. More than 10,000 people participated in this uprising.

[24] This strike took place from 5 August to 12 August (1953) when a committee of Force Ouvriére militants at a Bourdeaux PTT (Postes, Telephone, Telegraphe) office launched a protest against the Laniel government's attempt to cut public sector workers' salaries and retirement benefits. This strike paralyzed the mail, telephonic communications, and all public transportation.

[25] These refer to workers' manifestations against labor conditions imposed by their governments. The claims of the Hungarian revolt were mainly for self-management in productive units, reduction of inequalities among labor wages, control over planning processes, a new government composition, and a new orientation of the foreign policy.

[26] This was first indicated in *SB* No. 12, "Note sur la Situation Internationale," and later on in 1954 in "Situation de l'Impérialisme et Perspectives du Prolétariat," in *SB* No. 14 (April 1954).

[27] As noted previously, some years later in Castoriadis' work, autonomy would become an important concept reworked in the light of psychoanalysis.

[28] These issues were published in *SB* No. 13 and No. 14.

[29] The most detailed analysis about this crisis was published in *SB* No. 21.

[30] These elaborations were exposed in *SB* Nos. 13, 14, and 20.

[31] Further elaborations about this topic were published in English as "On the Content of Socialism I and II" in *Political and Social Writing*, Vols. 1 and 2.

[32] "Sur le Contenu du Socialisme I" was published in *SB* No. 17 (July 1955); "Sur le Contenu du Socialisme II" was published in *SB* No. 22 (July 1957); and "Sur le Contenu du Socialisme III: La Lutte des Ouvriers Contre l'Organisation de l'Entreprise Capitaliste" was published in *SB* No. 23 (January 1958). For English translations, see (Castoriadis, 1997k and 1997l).

[33] Smith (2010, p. 173) identifies four stages in Castoriadis' move from socialism to autonomy from 1955 to 1979.

[34] What the Algerian War meant for SouB, and the position of the group before colonial relations will be addressed in more detail later on.

[35] This position was argued by Castoriadis in *SB* No. 31 (December 1960), No. 32 (April 1961), and No. 33 (December 1961). These texts were reprinted as *Le Mouvement Revolutionnaire sous le Capitalisme Moderne* (vols. I, II, and III) and in *Political and Social Writings, Vol. 2. 1955-1960: From the Workers' Struggle Against Bureaucracy to Resolution in the Age of Modern Capitalism* (Castoriadis, 1988c).

Chapter 2

[1] Whitebook (1998, p. 143) notes that one of the major symptoms of our times is the abstract negation of Cartesianism with the rush into intersubjectivity.... Whether it emanates from Lévi-Strauss and structuralism, or from Wittgenstein and Habermas, the attempt has been to absorb the individual into the transindividual—the subjective into the intersubjective—so thoroughly that the moment of privatistic individuality drops out almost completely [resulting] in a superficial view of human creativity.

[2] It is important to note that Castoriadis does not equate radical imagination to the unconscious.

[3] For example, when Freud explained the Oedipal Complex he traced it back to the murder of the primal father. All his developments on the original phantasies followed this sort of theoretical path, induced by his positivistic intention of making psychoanalysis a formal science.

4 Freud makes this observation in his letters to Fliess dated on May 2, 1897 and May 25, 1897 (Masson, 1985).
5 Although later in his theory about sexual development Freud called heterosexuality the "normal" state of human sexuality, there is no doubt that he intended to change the conventional moral perception of homosexuality.
6 Dreams are characterized by overdetermination (meaning that a signifier always points to several signifieds), as well as by underdetermination (a signifier is not the only one possible for any signified) and oversymbolization (a signified can be indicated by several signifiers) (Castoriadis, 1992, p. 9).
7 For example, Freud's initial belief in the positive reality of the event that corresponds to the traumatic memory of neurotics, or his initial treatment of the topic of seduction scenes of a child by an adult, or the search for the primal scene as a real event (Castoriadis, 1987, p. 281).
8 This predominance is connected to what Freud calls the magical omnipotence of thought within the unconscious where if a desire arises the representation that fulfills it also appears. This is not to say that the organ pleasure dimension disappears.
9 See for example Castoriadis' discussions with Francisco Varela on the living-being and biology in "Life and Creation: Cornelius Castoriadis in Dialogue with Francisco Varela" (Castoriadis, 2011).
10 Castoriadis proposes an original process to explain the stratification of the human psyche, explained in more detail in Chapter 6 of *The Imaginary Institutions of Society*. Without doing justice to its complexity, I will only make brief reference to the different stages involved in such process centering on its most original and controversial aspects.
11 As discussed in the following chapter the monad concept can be highly controversial. For example, Laplanche (1986) observes that it is not possible to think about a primary unrepressed unconscious in psychoanalytical theory. In his eyes this would be equivalent to posing a false statement about the place of the biological dimension. For him it is through the original repression that the unconscious is constituted.
12 It is important to remember that the psyche will never lose the tendency to lock everything up in order to return to an impossible monadic state—and when it fails to do so, will appeal to its substitutes: hallucinatory satisfaction and phantasy.
13 Castoriadis also used the term libido formandi as specific to the human domain (1997b, p. 342).
14 As said, Castoriadis does not establish an absolute polarity between the individual and society. The individual or subject, as well as any form of intersubjectivity, are already social.
15 This is what Castoriadis calls closure. The term closure here is given the very precise meaning it enjoys in algebra. An algebraic field is said to be closed when every algebraic equation that can be written in this field, with the elements of this field, can be solved with elements from the same field (1997d, p. 87).
16 Castoriadis also considers ruptures to closure in Western Europe in the eleventh century, with the creation of communes that vindicated forms of auto-government, the renaissance, the workers' movements, and other movements, such as those of feminists and ecologists (Castoriadis, 1997a, pp. 103–27).

17 The term "discourse" cannot be taken in its narrow sense. It implies representational and affective referrals that make up the world into which the psyche is socialized.
18 Deliberative activity and self-reflection does not suppose or mean in Castoriadis the goal of becoming self-transparent. It is impossible for an individual to become so given the existence of the unconscious. Therefore conscious and unconscious activities are indissociable.
19 This does not mean that the radical imaginary does not count in the exercise of autonomy. It is understood here that there could not be autonomy without the explicit exercise of the radical imaginary.
20 Castoriadis also understands psychoanalysis as an activity that promotes the emergence of reflexive and deliberative subjectivities. For him this is the end and the goal of analysis.

Chapter 3

1 See J. Bernstein's analysis of Habermas' critiques of Castoriadis (Bernstein, 1989).
2 I will return to this discussion and its relationship to democracy later on addressing the notion of popular sovereignty and its relationship to autonomy.
3 It would not be exactly correct to define radical imagination as the point of origin of cultural representation, since for Castoriadis understanding the emergence of a creation or a new stratum in the totality of the existing-being is not about establishing "origins" or exact inaugural moments. It is about understanding the advent of something completely new; in this sense, the creation of meaning entails an essential fragmentation of total Being/being given in a magmatic order as explained in Chapter 2.
4 Noesis is the particular intentional act itself; a noema (plural, noemata) comprises all that which makes the act to be as if it were of an object experienced in a certain way (Mautner, 1998).
5 There has always been and always will be a dimension of the social institution in charge of this essential function: to reestablish order, to ensure the life and operation of society against whatever, actually or potentially, endangers them. This fact is one of the roots of explicit power (Castoriadis, 1991c, p. 154).
6 Castoriadis presented and responded to the observations of these authors in an interesting discussion in "Done and to be Done" (1997c, pp. 385–98).
7 Kalyvas (1998a, p. 162) is right when he notes that Castoriadis only provides good reasons to prefer the value of autonomy as a normative standard.
8 A more extended discussion about meaning and validity can be found in "Done and to be Done" (Castoriadis, 1997c, pp. 385–98).
9 Kalyvas (1998a, p. 168) has called attention to this issue, suggesting that the redefinition of the encounter between norm and fact enables us to understand the tensions present in Castoriadis between facticity and validity.
10 I will discuss here only the main theoretical intention of Arnason's project. His analyses are much comprehensive than the ones explored here, however, my interest lies in showing what I see as the principal theoretical difference from Castoriadis that reflects in their understandings of creation and history.

11 This framework studies the civilizations associated with the major world religions that provided the basis for divergent historical paths. Civilizations refer to the cultural modes of interpretation that first arrived with the onset of writing and which interacted with particular processes of state formation to produce distinct cultural complexes. Civilizations are perpetually self-transforming and develop not in isolation but through interaction with others. This civilizational analysis aims to identify common trends while avoiding, 1) the discredited evolutionary theory of western civilization as a universal normative standard, 2) the idea of distinct civilizations that develop in isolation from each other, and 3) notions of civilizations as engaged in a perpetual clash (Delanty, 2010, pp. 46–7).

12 For Adams (2005) a more moderate idea of creation is desirable. She states that the notion of *contextual creation* does not preclude the idea of creation sui generis and does not compromise the recognition of ontological novelty (p. 26).

13 Adams (2005, p. 35) states that Castoriadis does not acknowledge hermeneutical contributions because he associates this tradition with Gadamer and Heidegger and the with philosophical task of discerning an ultimate truth through interpretation, something that is at odds with his ideas of creation and autonomy.

14 Adams states that an aspect of Arnason's articulation of the world is the idea—drawing on Habermas—of mutual understanding. Where Habermas poses homogeneity to mutual understanding, Arnason is more interested in paying due respect to its heterogeneous modalities and intercultural aspects . . . the challenge is to rethink the idea of the "other"—and mutual understanding—such that there is neither the unbridgeable chasm of radical alterity nor the quashing of difference by the assimilation of the same (2007, p. 58).

15 Smith (2010) makes a parallel between Cornelius Castoriadis' and Charles Taylor's inquires into the philosophical questions: Who am I? Who are we? And how are we to live? By identifying their commonalities and differences, Smith moves beyond these authors to build his own arguments about these perennial questions.

16 This will be discussed later when the questions of representation, meaning, and the body are approached.

17 Smith (2010) refers to the term "oblique autonomy" discussed by Adams in a 2006 conference paper.

18 Castoriadis notes that this distinction makes sense, abstractly speaking, for all societies. It permits the interpretation of societies according to the distinction or articulation they institute among these three.

19 Castoriadis acknowledges here the obvious difference in scale between the Athenian democracy and contemporary democracies. He dismisses as "sophisms" all arguments against direct democracies based on issues of numbers or dimension, arguing that it could be possible to instaurate direct regimes in cities of 40,000–50,000 inhabitants, as Athenians did during the classical period.

20 Castoriadis accepts the Greek notion of "magistrates" that, as delegates, would be taking care of the division of political tasks—not the division of political labor in direct regimes, however, he does not elaborate on this issue to demonstrate how and why these cannot be assumed as a form of representation (1997c, pp. 407).

Chapter 4

[1] Whitebook, J. (unpublished manuscript) states that there are two possible ways to look at Foucault's developments over time. The first one claims that Foucault's career consisted in a series of radical breaks that tend to be seen as a product of his intellectual flexibility, open-mindedness, self-critical honesty, or in a few cases, as attempts to resolve theoretical problems he confronted. The second one—the one Whitebook subscribes to—argues that the series of radical breaks in the development of Foucault's career are more apparent than real, and that they are in fact generated by the foundational position he defended in "*Madness and Civilization*" that overvalued a romantic-transgressive thesis that he never gave up completely. In this sense, Foucault's radical breaks are only apparent, and they really represent an attempt to escape the inconsistencies generated by his continuing adherence to a transgressive approach reflected in his view on power, normality, and pathology.

[2] In relation to the idea of historical discontinuity, Foucault was influenced early on by Georges Canguilhem, who developed a new structural history of science that stated that science did not progress by gradual evolution, but involved a series of discontinuities.

[3] An interesting article by Bob Jessop (2006) argued that despite Foucault's explicit rejection of Marxism, papers such as "Society Must Be Defended," "Securité, Territoire, Population" (1977), and "Naissance de la Biopolitique" (1978) marked a turn on issues of governmentality where this position is attenuated and it is possible to identify resonances between him and Marx.

[4] According to an unpublished interview with the author by Enrique Escobar (Paris, 2003), Castoriadis never denied the role of power in society nor sought to theorize a powerless social formation. He declared himself surprised at being attentively read by some anarchists since, as he said, he never agreed with their position regarding power (Escobar, 2003).

[5] See the following articles by Castoriadis: "The Crisis of Culture and the State" (1991a), "Reflections on 'Rationality' and 'Development'" (1991e), "The Institution of Society and Religion" (1997h), and "Reflections on Racism" (1997s).

Chapter 5

[1] Unpublished manuscript by Joel Whitebook.

[2] Whitebook (*n.d.*) saw Foucault's position toward Freud as an ambivalent, never entirely resolved tension. According to him, Foucault initially praised the founder of psychoanalysis for having been the first to re-establish the dialogue with unreason after the Great Confinement. However, Foucault could not develop a systematic relationship with psychoanalysis because it conflicted with his temptation to valorize transgression. Despite Foucault's intellectual sophistication and early insights into the need to theoretically articulate an extra-discursive dimension, he never addressed this question, which generated inconsistencies in his work.

[3] *Ibid.*, pp. 37–40.

[4] *Ibid.*, p. 38.
[5] Klooger (2009, p. 111) added interesting observations about the idea of "leaning-on" in Castoriadis and proposed "a general division of the concept" that would differentiate the relationships between psyche and body and psyche and society on one hand, and between self and environment on the other.
[6] The idea of anaclisis was introduced by Freud to describe the original relationship, in the young child, between the sexual drives and the self-preservative functions. Arising from a specific site in the organism (an erotogenic zone), the sexual drives at first prop themselves on the self-preservative functions, and only later become independent. The self-preservative function thus sometimes offers its own object to the sexual drive; this is what Freud calls "anaclitic object-choice."

Like the notion of "deferred action" (*Nachträglichkeit*), that of "anaclisis" or "leaning-on" or "propping" (*Anlehnung*) constitutes a major theoretical concept that always remained latent in Freud's own work. . . . The German substantive *Anlehnung* is derived from the verb *Sichanlehnung*, meaning to "lean on" or "prop oneself on" . . . .What it describes is the support that sexuality derives, at the beginning, from various functions and bodily zones related to self-preservation: the mouth, the anus, the musculature, and so on. It is thus intimately bound up with the Freudian conception of infantile and adult sexuality as a much-broadened sphere, far more comprehensive than the genital alone, and indeed extending to the entire body.

The notion made its appearance in the first edition of "Three Essays on the Theory of Sexuality" . . . and was further explicated in later revisions of that work(Laplanche, n.d.).

Bibliography

Adams, S. (2005), 'Interpreting creation: Castoriadis and the birth of autonomy', *Thesis Eleven*, 83, 25–41.
—. (2007), 'Castoriadis and the permanent riddle of the world: changing configurations of worldliness and world alienation', *Thesis Eleven*, 90, 44–60.
—. (2011), *Castoriadis's Ontology: Being and Creation*. New York: Fordham University Press.
Aglietta, M. (1987), *A Theory of Capitalist Regulation*. London: Verso.
Arnason, J. (1989), 'The imaginary constitution of modernity', in G. Busino (ed.), *Revue Européenne des Sciences Sociales*, XXVII-86, 323–37.
—. (1994), 'Reason, imagination, interpretation', in G. Robinson and J. Rundell (eds), *Rethinking Imagination: Culture and Creativity*. London: Routledge, pp. 155–70.
—. (1997), 'World interpretation and mutual understanding', in A. Honneth, T. McCarthy, C. Offe and A. Wellmer (eds), *Cultural Political Interventions in the Unfinished Project of Enlightenment*. Cambridge, MA: MIT Press, pp. 247–69.
—. (2001), 'Autonomy and axiality: comparative perspectives on the Greek breakthrough', in J. Arnason and P. Murphy (eds), *Agon, Logos, Polis: The Greek Achievement and Its Aftermath*. Stuttgart: Franz Steiner, pp. 155–206.
—. (2003), *Civilizations in Dispute: Historical Questions and Theoretical Traditions*. Leiden and Boston: Brill.
—. (2011), 'Response to comments and criticisms', *European Journal of Social Theory*, 14, 107–18.
Bernauer, J. W. and Mahon, M. (2005), 'Michel Foucault's ethical imagination', in G. Gutting (ed.), *The Cambridge Companion to Foucault* (2nd edn). Cambridge: Cambridge University Press, pp. 149–76.
Bernstein, J. (1989), 'Praxis and aporia: Habermas's critique of Castoriadis', in G. Busino (ed.), *Autonomie et Autotransformation de la Société: La Philosophie Militante de Cornelius Castoriadis*. Génève: Librairie Droz, pp. 111–23.
Bernstein, J. (1995), *Recovering Ethical Life*. London: Routledge.
Bernstein, R. (1984), 'Foucault: critique as a philosophical ethos', in M. Kelly (ed.), *Critique and Power: Recasting the Foucault/Habermas Debate*. Cambridge, MA: MIT Press, pp. 211–41.
Best, S. and Kellner, D. (1991), *Postmodern Theory: Critical Interrogations*. New York: The Guilford Press.
Boschetti, A. (1988), *The Intellectual Enterprise: Sartre and Les Temps Modernes*. Evanston: Northwestern University Press.
Bourdieu, P. (1993), *Sociology in Question*. London: Sage.
Ciaramelli, F. (1997), 'Self-presupposition of the origin: homage to Cornelius Castoriadis', *Thesis Eleven*, 49, 45–67.

Cohen, J. (2005), 'The self-institution of society and representative government: can the circle be squared?', *Thesis Eleven*, 80, 9–37.

Cohn-Bendit, D. (1968), 'The March 22nd movement', in *The French Student Revolt: The Leaders Speak*. New York: Hill and Wang, pp. 48–60.

Curtis, D. A. (1988), 'Foreword', in C. Castoriadis (ed.), *Political and Social Writings, Vol. 1: 1946–1955: From the Critique of Bureaucracy to the Positive Content of Socialism*. Minneapolis: University of Minnesota Press.

—. (1997a), 'Foreword', in D. A. Curtis (ed.), *The Castoriadis Reader*. Oxford: Blackwell Publishers, pp. vii–xv.

—. (1997b), 'Translator's foreword', in D. A. Curtis (ed.), *World in Fragments: Writings on Politics, Society, Psychoanalysis and Imagination*. Stanford: Stanford University Press, pp. xi–xxx.

Davidson, A. (2005), 'Ethics as ascetics: Foucault, the history of ethics and ancient thought', in G. Gutting (ed.), *The Cambridge Companion to Foucault* (2nd edn). Cambridge: Cambridge University Press, pp. 123–49.

Delanty, G. (2010), 'Civilizational analysis and critical theory', *Thesis Eleven*, 100, 46–52.

Dews, P. (1984), 'Power and subjectivity in Foucault', *New Left Review*, 144, 72–95.

—. (1987), *Logics of Disintegration*. London: Verso.

—. (1989), 'The return of the subject in late Foucault', *Radical Philosophy*, 51, 37–40.

—. (1995), *The Limits of Disenchantment: Essays on Contemporary European Philosophy*. London: Verso.

Dosse, F. (1997), *The History of Structuralism: The Signs Sets, 1967-Present* (Vol. 2). Minneapolis: University of Minnesota Press.

Dreyfus, H. and Rabinow, P. (1983), *Michel Foucault: Beyond Structuralism and Hermeneutics* (2nd edn). Chicago: University of Chicago Press.

Eisenstadt, S. N. (ed.) (1986), *The Origins and Diversity of the Axial Civilizations*. New York: SUNY Press.

—. (2001), 'The civilizational dimension of modernity', *International Sociology*, 16(3), 320–40.

—. (2003), *Comparative Civilizations and Multiple Modernities* (Vols 1 and 2). Leiden: Brill.

Eribon, D. (1991), *Michel Foucault*. Cambridge: Harvard University Press.

Escobar, E. (2003), *Interview with Marcela Tovar-Restrepo*. Unpublished manuscript.

Escobar, E. and Vernay, P. (2002), 'Postface', in E. Escobar, P. Vernay and M. Gondicas (eds), *Sujet et Vérité: Dans le Monde Social-Historique: Séminaires 1986–1987. La Création Humaine l*. Paris: Éd Seuil.

Fraser, N. (1989), *Unruly Practices*. Minneapolis: University of Minnesota Press.

Freud, S. (1962), *Three Essays on the Theory of Sexuality*. New York: Basic Books.

—. (1965), *The Interpretation of the Dreams*. New York: Avon Books.

—. (1984), *The Neuro-Psychoses of Defence*. The Standard Edition of the Complete Psychological Works of Sigmund Freud, Vol III (1893–1899): Early Psycho-Analytic Publications. London: Hogarth, pp. 41–61.

Fryer, P. (2000), The Hungarian Tragedy 1956. viewed Oct 30, 2009 hppt://www.Hungary1956/webcom.

Gottraux, P. (1997), *Socialisme ou Barbarie: Un Engagement Politique et Intellectuel dans la france de l'Après-guerre*. Lausanne: Éd. Payot.

Gutting, G. (1994), 'Michel Foucault', in G. Gutting (ed.), *The Cambridge Companion to Foucault*. Cambridge: Cambridge Press, pp. 1–27.
—. (1998), 'Post-Structuralism in the social sciences', in *Encyclopedia of Philosophy*. London: Routledge.
Habermas, J. (1987), *The Philosophical Discourse of Modernity*. Cambridge, MA: MIT Press.
—. (1992), 'Individuation through socialization: on George Herbert Mead's theory of subjectivity', in C. Morris (ed.), *Postmetaphysical Thinking: Philosophical Essays*. Cambridge, MA: MIT Press, pp. 149–204.
—. (1996), 'Labor and interaction: remarks on Hegel's Jena philosophy of mind', in J. O'Neil (ed.), *Hegel's Dialectic of Desire and Recognition*. New York: State University of New York Press, pp. 123–49.
Han, B. (2002), *Foucault's Critical Project: Between the Transcendental and the Historical*. Stanford: Stanford University Press.
Hastings-King, S. (1999), *Fordism and the Marxist revolutionary Project: A History of Socialisme ou Barbarie*. Ph.D. Dissertation, Cornell University.
Honneth, A. (1986), 'Rescuing the revolution with an ontology: on Cornelius Castoriadis' theory of society', *Thesis Eleven*, 14, 62–78.
—. (1998), 'Foucault's theory of society: a systems-theoretic dissolution of the dialectic of enlightenment', in M. Kelly (ed.) *Critique and Power: Recasting Foucault/Habermas Debate*. Cambridge, MA: MIT Press, pp. 157–85.
Jameson, F. (1972), *The Prison-House of Language: A Critical Account of Structuralism and Russian Formalism*. Princeton: Princeton University Press.
Jessop, B. (2006), 'From micro-powers to governmentality: Foucault's work on statehood, state formation, statecraft and state power', *Political Geography*, 26(1), 34–40.
Kalyvas, A. (1998a), 'Norm and critique in Castoriadis' theory of autonomy', *Constellations*, 5(2), 161–82.
—. (1998b), 'The radical instituting power and democratic theory', *Journal of the Hellenic Diaspora*, 24(1), 9–29.
—. (2002), 'Heteronomía, alienación ideología: Castoriadis y la cuestión de la dominación', *Archipielago*, 54, 76–84.
—. (2008), *Democracy and the Politics of the Extraordinary*. Cambridge: Cambridge University Press.
Klooger, J. (2009), *Castoriadis: Psyche, Society, Autonomy*. Leiden: Brill.
Kramer, M. (1996), 'Hungary and Poland, 1956: Khrushchev's CPSU CC Presidium Meeting on East European Crises, 24 October 1956', in Charles S. Maier (ed.), *The Cold War in Europe: The End of a Divided Continent* (3rd edn). Princeton, NJ: First Markus Wiener Publishers Inc., pp. 365–87.
Laplanche, J. (n.d.), 'Anaclisis/Anaclitic', *International Dictionary of Psychoanalysis*. Viewed 28 August 2011. http://www.enotes.com/psychoanalysis-encyclopedia/anaclisis-anaclitic.
—. (1986), 'La pulsion de mort dans la théorie de la pulsion sexuelle', in *La Pulsion de Mort*, Premier Symposium de la Fédération Européenne de Psychanalyse, PUF, 1986.
Laplanche, J. and Pontalis, J. (1993), *Diccionario de Psicoanálisis*. Barcelona: Editorial Labor.

Lefort, C. (1979), *Élements d'une Critique de la Bureaucratie*. Paris: Gallimard.
Lichtheim, G. (1966), *Marxism in Modern France*. New York: Columbia University Press.
Lipietz, A. (1996), 'Facing the danger of megapolization', in *Production, Use and Consumption of the City*. Bogotá: Editora Guadalupe.
Macey, D. (1995), *The Lives of Michel Foucault*. New York: Vintage Books.
Masson, J. M. (ed.) (1985), *The Complete Letters of Sigmund Freud to Wilhelm Fliess, 1887–1904*. Cambridge: Harvard University Press.
Mautner, T. (ed.) (1998), *The Penguin Dictionary of Philosophy*. London: Penguin.
Merquior, J. (1986), *From Prague to Paris: A Critique of Structuralism and Post-structuralist Thought*. London: Verso.
Molina, E. (1998), 'Socialismo o Barbarie: historia de un proyecto político', *Metapolítica*, 2(8), 721–42.
Mouffe, C. (2007), *Democracia y Relativismo: Debate con el Mauss*. M. Diaz (trans). Madrid: Ed. Minima Trotta.
Nussbaum, M. (1999), 'The Professor of Parody', *The New Republic*, 22 February 1999. Viewed 28 August 2011. http://www.akad.se/Nussbaum.pdf.
Poltier H. (1989), 'De la praxis a l'institution et de retour', in *Autonomie et Transformation: La Philosophie Militante de Cornelius Castoriadis*. Geneva: Librarie Droz, pp. 419–39.
Poster, M. (1975), *Existential Marxism in Postwar France: From Sartre to Althusser*. New Jersey: Princeton University Press.
Rabinow, P. (1984), 'Introduction', in P. Rabinow (ed.), *Foucault Reader*. New York: Pantheon Books.
—. (1994), 'Modern and counter-modern: ethos and epoch', in G. Gutting (ed.), *The Cambridge Companion to Foucault*. Cambridge: Cambridge University Press, pp. 197–215.
Rajchman, J. (1985), *Michel Foucault: The Freedom of Philosophy*. New York: Columbia University Press.
Ross, K. (1999), *Fast Cars, Clean Bodies: Decolonization and the Reordering of French Culture*. Cambridge, MA: MIT Press.
Said, E. (1994), 'Foucault and the imagination of power', in G. Gutting (ed.), *The Cambridge Companion to Foucault*. Cambridge: Cambridge University Press, pp. 149–55.
Sarup, M. (1993), *Post-Structuralism and Post-modernism*. Athens, GA: University of Georgia Press.
Schnapp, A. and Vidal-Naquet, P. (1971), *The French Student Uprising, November 1967–June 1968*. M. Jolas (trans). Boston: Beacon Press.
Simons, J. (1995), *Foucault and the Political (Thinking the Political)*. London: Routledge.
Sluga, H. (2005), 'Foucault's encounter with Heidegger and Nietzsche', in G. Gutting (ed.), *The Cambridge Companion to Foucault* (2nd edn). Cambridge: Cambridge University Press, pp. 210–40.
Smith, K. E. (2010), *Meaning, Subjectivity, Society: Making Sense of Modernity*. Leiden and Boston: Brill.
Taylor, C. (1979), *Hegel and Modern Society*. Cambridge: Cambridge University Press.
Visker, R. (1995), *Michel Foucault: Genealogy as a Critique*. London: Verso.
Walzer, M. (1983), 'The politics of Michel Foucault', *Dissent*, 30, 481–90.

Whitebook, J. (1995), *Perversion and Utopia*. Cambridge, MA: MIT Press.
—. (1998), 'Requiem for a selbstdenker: Cornelius Castoriadis (1922–1997)', *Constellations*, 5(2), 143–60.
—. (2005), 'Against interiority: Foucault's struggle with psychoanalysis', in G. Gutting (ed.), *The Cambridge Companion to Foucault* (2nd edn). Cambridge: Cambridge University Press, pp. 312–47.
—. (2010a), *Against Freud: Foucault's Struggle with Psychoanalysis*. Unpublished manuscript.
—. (2010b), 'The hermeneutics of suspicion reconsidered', in S. Gourgouris (ed.), *Freud and Fundamentalism*. New York: Fordham University Press, pp. 166–81.
Williams, C. (2001), *Contemporary French Philosophy: Modernity and the Resistance of the Subject*. London: The Athlone Press.

Foucault References

Foucault, M. (1970), *The Order of Things: An Archaeology of the Human Sciences*. New York: Pantheon Books.
—. (1972), *The Archaeology of Knowledge*. A. Sheridan (trans). New York: Pantheon Books.
—. (1973a), *Madness and Civilization: A History of Insanity in the Age of Reason*. R. Howard (trans). New York: Vintage Books.
—. (1973b), *The Birth of Clinic*. A. Sheridan (trans). New York: Pantheon Books.
—. (1977), *Language, Counter-Memory, Practice*. D. Bouchard (ed.), D. Bouchard and S. Simon (trans). Ithaca, NY: Cornell University Press.
—. (1978), *The History of Sexuality, Vol. 1: An Introduction*. R. Hurley (trans). New York: Pantheon Books.
—. (1979), *Discipline and Punish*. A. Sheridan (trans). New York: Vintage Books.
—. (1980), *Power/Knowledge: Selected Interviews and Other Writings*. C. Gordon, L. Marshall, J. Mepham and K. Spoer (eds), C. Gordon (trans). New York: Pantheon Books.
—. (1983a), 'Structuralism and post-structuralism: an interview with Michel Foucault', *Telos*, 55, 195–211.
—. (1983b), 'The subject and power', in H. Dreyfus and P. Rabinow (eds), *Michel Foucault: Beyond Structuralism and Hermeneutics*. Chicago: University of Chicago Press, pp. 208–26.
—. (1984), 'What is enlightenment?', in P. Rabinow (ed.), *The Foucault Reader*. C. Porter (trans). New York: Pantheon.
—. (1985), *The Use of Pleasure, Volume 2 of History of Sexuality*. R. Hurley (trans). New York: Pantheon Books.
—. [1966] (1988a), *Las Palabras y las Cosas*. México City: Siglo XXI.
—. (1988b), 'Power and Sex', in L. D. Kritzman (ed.), *Michel Foucault: Politics, Philosophy, Culture: Interviews and Other Writings*. A. Sheridan (trans). New York: Routledge.
—. (1988c), 'Technologies of the self', in L. H. Martin, H. Gutman and P. H. Hutton (eds), *Technologies of the Self: A Seminar with Michel Foucault*. Amherst: University of Massachusetts Press.

—. (1993), 'An introduction to Ludwig Binswanger's "Dreams and Existence"', F. Williams (trans), in M. Foucault, and L. Binswanger, *Dreams and Existence*. K. Hoeller (ed.). Atlantic Highlands, NJ: Humanities Press International, Inc. pp. 31–81.

—. (1994), 'The ethic of care of the self as a practice of freedom', in J. Bernauer and D. Rasmussen (eds), *The Final Foucault*. Cambridge: MIT Press.

Castoriadis References

Castoriadis, C. [1953] (1976a), 'Burocracia después de la muerte de Stalin', in *La Sociedad Burocrática* (Vol. 2). E. Escobar (trans). Barcelona: Tusquets Editores, pp. 127–53.

—. [1957] (1976b), 'La vía polaca hacia la burocracia', in *La Sociedad Burocrática* (Vol. 2). E. Escobar (trans). Barcelona: Tusquets Editores, pp. 273–301.

—. [1957] (1979a), 'Balance, perspectivas, tareas', in E. Escobar (trans), *La Experiencia del Movimiento Obrero* (Vol. 1). Barcelona: Tusquets Editores, pp. 287–305.

—. [1973] (1979b), 'Introducción. La cuestión de la historia del movimiento obrero', in *La Experiencia del Movimiento Obrero* (Vol. 1). E. Escobar (trans). Barcelona: Tusquets Editores, pp. 9–89.

—. [1974] (1979c), *La Experiencia del Movimiento Obrero* (Vol. 1). *Como Luchar*. Barcelona: Tusquets Editores.

—. [1949–1952] (1979d), 'Nota final a "el partido revolucionario" y a la "dirección proletaria"', in E. Escobar (trans), *La Experiencia del Movimiento Obrero* (Vol. 1). Barcelona: Tusquets Editores, pp. 131–45.

—. [1949] (1979e), 'El partido revolucionario', in E. Escobar (trans), *La Experiencia del Movimiento Obrero* (Vol. 1). Barcelona: Tusquets Editores, pp. 119–31.

—. [1967] (1979f), 'Suspensión de la publicación de Socialisme ou Barbarie', in E. Escobar (trans), *La Experiencia del Movimiento Obrero* (Vol. 2). Barcelona: Tusquets Editores, pp. 311–17.

—. [1975] (1983), *La Institución Imaginaria de la Sociedad*. M. A. Galmarini (trans). Madrid: Tusquets Editores.

—. [1972] (1984a), 'Modern science and philosophical interrogation', in *Crossroads in the Labyrinth*. Cambridge: MIT Press.

—. [1971] (1984b), 'The sayable and the unsayable: homage to Merleau-Ponty', in K. Soper and M. H. Ryle (trans, eds), *Crossroads in the Labyrinth*. Brighton: Harvester Press, pp. 119–44.

—. [1975] (1987), *The Imaginary Institution of Society*. K. Blamey (trans). Cambridge, MA: MIT Press.

—. [1949] (1988a), 'The concentration of forces of production', in D. A. Curtis (trans, ed.), *Political and Social Writings, Vol. 1. 1946–1955: From the Critique of Bureaucracy to the Positive Content of Socialism*. Minneapolis: University of Minnesota Press, pp. 67–76.

—. [1955] (1988b), 'Content of socialism I', in D. A. Curtis (trans, ed.), *Political and Social Writings, Vol. 1. 1946–1955: From the Critique of Bureaucracy to the Positive Content of Socialism*. Minneapolis: University of Minnesota Press, pp. 290–313.

—. (1988c), 'Modern Capitalism and Revolution', in D. A. Curtis (trans, ed.), *Political and Social Writings, Vol. 2. 1955–1960: From the Workers' Struggle Against Bureaucracy to Resolution in the Age of Modern Capitalism.* Minneapolis: University of Minnesota Press, pp. 226–316.

—. (1988d), *Political and Social Writings, Vol. 1. 1946–1955: From the Critique of Bureaucracy to the Positive Content of Socialism.* D. A. Curtis (trans, ed.). Minneapolis: University of Minnesota Press.

—. [1947] (1988e), 'The problem of USSR and the possibility of a third historical solution', in D. A. Curtis (trans, ed.), *Political and Social Writings, Vol. 1. 1946–1955: From the Critique of Bureaucracy to the Positive Content of Socialism.* Minneapolis: University of Minnesota Press, pp. 44–56.

—. [1952] (1988f), 'Proletarian leadership', in D. A. Curtis (trans, ed.), *Political and Social Writings, Vol. 1. 1946–1955: From the Critique of Bureaucracy to the Positive Content of Socialism.* Minneapolis: University of Minnesota Press, pp. 198–205.

—. [1956] (1988g), 'Proletarian revolution against bureaucracy', in D. A. Curtis (trans, ed.), *Political and Social Writings, Vol. 2. 1955–1960: From the Workers' Struggle Against Bureaucracy to Resolution in the Age of Modern Capitalism.* Minneapolis: University of Minnesota Press, pp. 57–90.

—. [1954] (1988h), 'Situation of imperialism and proletarian perspective', in D. A. Curtis (trans, ed.), *Political and Social Writings, Vol. 1. 1946–1955: From the Critique of Bureaucracy to the Positive Content of Socialism.* Minneapolis: University of Minnesota Press, pp. 256–90.

—. [1949] (1988i), 'Socialism or barbarism', in D. A. Curtis (trans, ed.), *Political and Social Writings, Vol. 1. 1946–1955: From the Critique of Bureaucracy to the Positive Content of Socialism.* Minneapolis: University of Minnesota Press, pp. 76–107.

—. [1986] (1989), 'The state of the subject today', *American Imago*, 46, 371–412.

—. (1991a), 'The crisis of culture and the state', in D. A. Curtis (trans, ed.), *Philosophy, Politics, Autonomy: Essays in Political Philosophy.* New York: Oxford University Press, pp. 219–43.

—. [1983] (1991b), 'Greek *polis* and the creation of democracy', in D. A. Curtis (trans, ed.), *Philosophy, Politics, Autonomy: Essays in Political Philosophy.* New York: Oxford University Press, pp. 81–124.

—. [1988] (1991c), 'Individual, society, rationality, history', in D. A. Curtis (trans, ed.), *Philosophy, Politics, Autonomy: Essays in Political Philosophy.* New York: Oxford University Press, pp. 47–81. By permission of Oxford University Press, Inc.

—. [1974] (1991d), 'Power, politics and autonomy', in D. A. Curtis (ed.), *Philosophy, Politics, Autonomy: Essays in Political Philosophy.* New York: Oxford University Press, pp. 143–74.

—. [1974] (1991e), 'Reflections on "rationality" and "development"', in D. A. Curtis (ed.), *Philosophy, Politics, Autonomy: Essays in Political Philosophy.* New York: Oxford University Press, pp. 175–219.

—. (1991f), 'The social-historical: mode of being, problems of knowledge in philosophy, politics and autonomy', in D. A. Curtis (trans, ed.), *Philosophy, Politics, Autonomy: Essays in Political Philosophy.* New York: Oxford University Press, pp. 33–46.

—. [1991] (1992), 'Logic, imagination, reflection', *American Imago*, 49, 3–33.

—. [1977] (1993a), *Political and Social Writings, Vol. 3. 1961–1979. Recommencing the Revolution: From Socialism to the Autonomous Society.* D. A. Curtis (trans, ed.), Minneapolis: University of Minnesota Press.

—. (1993b), 'Merleau-Ponty and the Weight of the Ontological Tradition', D. A. Curtis (trans), *Thesis Eleven*, 36, 1–36.

—. (1993c), 'Subjetividad e histórico-social', *Zona Erógena*, 15, 12–21.

—. [1991] (1997a), 'El avance de la insignificancia', in A. Pignato (trans), *El Avance de la Insignificancia*. Buenos Aires: Eudeba, pp. 75–103.

—. [1994] (1997b), 'Culture in a democratic society', in D. A. Curtis (trans, ed.), *The Castoriadis Reader*. Oxford: Blackwell Publishers, pp. 338–49.

—. [1989] (1997c), 'Done and to be done', in D. A. Curtis (trans, ed.), *The Castoriadis Reader*. Oxford: Blackwell Publishers, pp. 361–418.

—. [1991] (1997d), 'The Greek and the modern political imaginary', in D. A. Curtis (trans, ed.), *World in Fragments: Writings on Politics, Society, Psychoanalysis and Imagination*. Stanford: Stanford University Press, pp. 84–108.

—. [1991] (1997e), 'Imaginación, imaginario, reflexión', in *Ontología de la Creación*. Bogotá: Ensayo y Error, pp. 131–213.

—. [1991] (1997f), 'Interview with Oliver Mongin, Joel Roman and Ramin Jahabegloo: El Deterioro de Occidente', in A. Pignato (trans), *El Avance de la Insignificancia*. Buenos Aires: Eudeba, pp. 75–103.

—. [1981] (1997g), 'The imaginary: creation in the social-historical domain', in D. A. Curtis (trans, ed.), *World in Fragments: Writings on Politics, Society, Psychoanalysis and Imagination*. Stanford: Stanford University Press, pp. 3–19.

—. [1982] (1997h), 'Institution of society and religion', in D. A. Curtis (trans, ed.), *World in Fragments: Writings on Politics, Society, Psychoanalysis and Imagination*. Stanford: Stanford University Press, pp. 311–31.

—. [1988] (1997i), 'Logic, imagination, reflection', in D. A. Curtis (trans, ed.), *World in Fragments: Writings on Politics, Society, Psychoanalysis and Imagination*. Stanford: Stanford University Press, pp. 311–31.

—. [1989] (1997j), 'The logic of magmas and the question of autonomy', in D. A. Curtis (trans, ed.), *The Castoriadis Reader*. Oxford: Blackwell Publishers, pp. 290–319.

—. [1955] (1997k), 'On the content of socialism (1955–1957): Excerpts', in D. A. Curtis (trans, ed.), *The Castoriadis Reader*. Oxford: Blackwell Publishers, pp. 40–9.

—. [1957] (1997l), 'On the content of socialism, II', in D. A. Curtis (trans, ed.), *The Castoriadis Reader*. Oxford: Blackwell Publishers, pp. 49–106.

—. [1974] (1997m), ' "The only way to find out if you can swim is to get into the water": an introductory interview', in D. A. Curtis (trans, ed.), *The Castoriadis Reader*. Oxford: Blackwell Publishers, pp. 1–35.

—. [1988] (1997n), 'Phusis and autonomy', in D. A. Curtis (trans, ed.), *World in Fragments: Writings on Politics, Society, Psychoanalysis and Imagination*. Stanford: Stanford University Press, pp. 331–42.

—. [1949] (1997o), 'Presentation of Socialisme ou Barbarie: an organ of critique and revolutionary orientation', in D. A. Curtis (trans, ed.), *The Castoriadis Reader*. Oxford: Blackwell Publishers, pp. 35–40.

—. [1996] (1997p), 'Psychoanalysis and philosophy', in D. A. Curtis (trans, ed.), *The Castoriadis Reader*. Oxford: Blackwell Publishers, pp. 349–61.

—. (1997q), 'Psychoanalysis and politics', in D. A. Curtis (trans, ed.), *World in Fragments: Writings on Politics, Society, Psychoanalysis and Imagination.* Stanford: Stanford University Press, pp. 125–36.

—. [1994] (1997r), 'Radical imagination and the social instituting imaginary', in D. A. Curtis (trans, ed.), *The Castoriadis Reader.* Oxford: Blackwell Publishers, pp. 319–38.

—. (1997s), 'Reflections on racism', in D. A. Curtis (trans, ed.), *World in Fragments: Writings on Politics, Society, Psychoanalysis and Imagination.* Stanford: Stanford University Press, pp. 19–32.

—. [1992] (1997t), 'The retreat from autonomy: postmodernism as generalized conformism', in D. A. Curtis (trans, ed.), *World in Fragments: Writings on Politics, Society, Psychoanalysis and Imagination.* Stanford: Stanford University Press, pp. 32–47.

—. [1976] (2000a), 'La Fuente Húngara', in D. Monteira (trans), *La Exigencia Revolucionaria.* Madrid: Acuarela Libros, pp. 75–119.

—. [1976] (2000b), 'Transformación social y creación', in D. Monteira (trans), *La Exigencia Revolucionaria.* Madrid: Acuarela Libros, pp. 199–224.

—. (2007), *Democracia y Relativismo: Debate con el Mauss.* M. Diaz (trans). Madrid: Ed. Minima Trotta.

—. [1993] (2010a), 'The Contribution of Psychoanalysis to Understanding the Genesis of Society', in S. Gourgouris (trans, ed.), *Freud and Fundamentalism.* New York: Fordham University Press, pp. 145–66.

—. (2010b), 'A society adrift', in H. Arnold (trans), *A Society Adrift: Interviews and Debates, 1974–1997.* New York: Fordham University Press, pp. 206–15.

—. (2010c), 'What political parties cannot do', in H. Arnold (trans), *A Society Adrift: Interviews and Debates, 1974–1997.* New York: Fordham University Press, pp. 117–25.

—. (2011), *Postscript on Insignificance: Dialogues with Cornelius Castoriadis.* G. Rockhill and J. V. Garner (trans). London, New York: Continnum Press.

Index

agency,
  democracy 90
  Foucault's notion of 134
  ontology of creation 33, 63
  self-agency 119, 121, 124
  SouB 32
  subject,
    Castoriadis formulation 66
    creative psychical capacity and society 70
    historical dimension 65–6
    radical imagination 66–7
    self-reflective capacity 70–1
    social-historical creation 67
anaclisis *see* leaning-on explanation theory
The Archaeology of Knowledge 98–100, 123
autogestion phase, SouB 13
  Algerian War 30
  Castoriadis theoretical analysis 31–2
  Gaullism 31
  Marxist theory, revisions of 31

The Birth of the Clinic 98
bureaucratic capitalism 12, 17–18, 21, 143n. 14

Castoriadis vs. Foucault,
  epistemological and political relativism 134
  Freud's work 135
  intersubjectivity 134
  main contribution 133
  meaning and representation 136
  political positions 137
  psychoanalysis 135–6
  role of theory 138

collective autonomy,
  politics and democracy 62
  society and history 61–2
counter-discourses 128

democracy,
  ancient Greek creation of 87
  contemporary 90
  direct 87–8
  instituted/instituting power 78–9, 88
  Paris Commune 89
  politics and political, distinction of 86–7
  representative 87
direct democracy 87–8
Discipline and Punish 101–2
dreams 39–41, 117–18, 145n. 6

Foucault's work,
  The Archaeology of Knowledge 98–100
  The Birth of the Clinic 98
  Discipline and Punish 101–2
  genealogical approach, power 101–4
  The History of Sexuality,
    bio-power 103
    discourse production 103–4
    subjectivity, shifts in 104
  Madness and Civilization 97–8
  The Order of Things 98–9
    episteme and discourse 95
  poststructuralism,
    aesthetics of existence 95
    enlightenment propositions 94
    episteme and discourse 95
    humanism 96–7
    language 92
    reality 92–3

subject 94–5
theory of discourse 93
truth 92, 95–6
power and emancipation 107
technologies of the self 105
types, technologies 104
French Fordism 2, 12, 28
French intellectual group *see* Socialisme ou Barbarie (SouB)

Gaullism 10, 31

Habermasian framework,
Castoriadis conception 69–71
process of socialization,
individual–society mediation 68
social individual, linguistic capacity 67–8
psyche and society 69–70
heteronomy *see also* social change
Castoriadis understanding 110–11
vs. homogeneity 58
instituting/instituted society 111
power and domination 110
social-historical dimension 139
society 58
The History of Sexuality,
bio-power 103
discourse production 103–4
subjectivity, shifts in 104
human psyche,
afunctionality 38–9
Castoriadis vs. Freud concepts 42–4
indetermination 39–41
society *see* imaginary social significations (ISS)
stratification,
leaning-on explanation, creation 50–2
monadic stage 48–9
Oedipal phase 49–50
psyche to society relation 52–4
sublimation process 48
triadic phase 49
Whitebook's criticism 50
human sexuality 38–9
The Hungarian Revolution 25, 27–8, 31

The Imaginary Institution of Society (IIS) 33
imaginary social significations (ISS),
definition 55
history 56
instituting power 74
legein and teukhein 56–7
magma of significations 55
magmatic and ensidic dimensions 57
social meaning 72
imperialism 18, 21, 31
individual autonomy,
conscious reflectiveness 60–1
democracy 87
Ego and Id 59
intersubjectivity 61
instituted society,
autonomous society 88
collective autonomy 62
heteronomy 58, 111
intersubjectivity 61
legein and teukhein 56–7, 73
social closure 75
instituting society,
autonomous society 88
change and innovation 73
collective autonomy 62
heteronomy 58, 111
social-historical 56
social meaning 73–4
intersubjectivity,
Castoriadis vs. Foucault 134
Freud's study 34
individual autonomy 61
political arena 122
ISS *see* imaginary social significations (ISS)

knowledge,
subject, structure, and inscription of 116

leaning-on explanation theory,
biological–social relationship 125
Habermasian position 68
idea of 149n. 6
living-being 67
society 54
stratification, human psyche 48
legein 56–7

Index

Le Tambour Café phase, SouB,
  bureaucratic capitalism 17–18
  Korean War 22
  Marxism 16
  revolutionary politics, proletarians 19
  Trotskyism 15

Madness and Civilization 97–8
magma 44
Marxist theory, revisions of 31

ontology of creation *see also* social change
  closed society,
    collective autonomy 61–2
    heteronomous 58
    individual autonomy 59–61
  contemporary theory, extremes of 33
  Freud's psychoanalytical findings 34–5
  radical imagination,
    Aristotle view 35–6
    definition 35
    foundations of 37–8
    historical omission of 36–7
    Kant's intuition 36
    ontological assumptions 37
    phantasy 41–5
    psychical representation 38–41
  social-historical dimension of society 34
  ISS 55–7
  social institutions (SI) 55
  strata, existing-being,
    for-itself 45–6
    heterogeneous 45
    human psyche 46
    individual and collective
      autonomy 47
    irreducible 45
    living-being 46
    social individual 46–7
    society and social-historical 47
  stratification, human psyche,
    force of formation 50–1
    leaning-on explanation, creation 50–2
    monadic stage 48–9
    Oedipal phase 49–50
    psyche to society relation 52–4
    sublimation process 48
    triadic phase 49
    Whitebook's criticism 50
The Order of Things 98–9
  episteme and discourse 95

phantasy 37–8 *see also* radical
    imagination
poststructuralism,
  aesthetics of existence 95
  enlightenment propositions 94
  episteme and discourse 95
  humanism 96–7
  language 92
  reality 92–3
  subject 94–5
  theory of discourse 93
  truth 92, 95–6
Pouvoir Ouvrier (PO) 11
power and domination,
  Castoriadis work,
    heteronomy 110–11
    institutions 110–12
  Foucault's theory,
    historical discontinuity 109
    Honneth view 108
    institutions 112
    ruptures of epistemes 109
    theorizing power 109

radical imagination,
  Aristotle view 35–6
  definition 35
  foundations of 37–8
  historical omission of 36–7
  Kant's intuition 36
  ontological assumptions 37
  phantasy,
    Castoriadis vs. Freud concepts 42–4
    magma 44
    unconscious logic 41–2
  psychical representation,
    afunctionality 38–9
    Castoriadis vs. Freud
      concepts 42–4
    indetermination 39–41
representative democracy 87
Russian bureaucracy 17–18

social change,
  Castoriadis' autonomy,
    Adams view 80–3
    Arnason view 79–83
    auto-reflection 78
    Ciaramelli's view 81
    civilizational axial age approach 80
    de jure validity 78
    democracy 78–9, 86–90
    hermeneutical transformation 80
    heteronomous society 75
    heteronomy 84–5
    Klooger view 79, 84
    legitimation 77, 79
    normative dimension 76–7, 130
    psychoanalytic theory 75
    relativism 77
    Smith view 82
  Castoriadis vs. Foucault 134, 137, 139
  defenses 74
  Foucault's work,
    normative criteria 129–30
    politics 127–8
    power 128–9
    resistance and counter-discourses 128
    subject 122
    Walzer view 131
  social-historical 74–5
social meaning,
  Castoriadis vs. Foucault 136
  Castoriadis' work,
    legein and teukhein, operations of 73
    magmatic organization 73
    psychical representation 125–6
    and representation 74
    social institutions 72
    stability 73–4
  Foucault's work,
    body and psyche 126
    discourse and power 123
    epistemic ruptures 123
    psychical representation 125
    psychoanalysis 127
    self-agency 124
    social practices 123–4
socialism,
  Castoriadis definition 12
  direct democracy, worker councils 24
  Hungarian Councils 26–8
  Polish crisis 25
  proletarian management 19
  self-management 18
  untouchable truths 14
  USSR 11–12, 17
Socialisme ou Barbarie (SouB)
  autogestion,
    Algerian War 30
    Castoriadis theoretical analysis 31–2
    Gaullism 31
    Marxist theory, revisions of 31
  capitalist organization 28–9
  content of socialism 29
  On the Content of Socialism (I, II, III) 28
  death of Stalin 23–4
  decentralized democracy 30
  East Berlin events 23–4
  Fordism, in France 12
  French strike 24
  initial work and issues 10–11
  Le Tambour Café,
    bureaucratic capitalism 17–18
    Korean War 22
    Marxism 16
    revolutionary politics, proletarians 19
    Trotskyism 15
  mistake acknowledgment, Korean War 23
  phases 13–14
  Polish crisis 25
  Pouvoir Ouvrier (PO) 11
  self-organization, working class 27
  Socialism Reaffirmed 142n. 12
  in USSR 11–12
  workers' councils, tradition of 12–13, 26
socialization, process of,
  individual–society mediation 68
  social individual, linguistic capacity 67–8
society,
  Being 140
  democracy 78, 86
  history 82–3
  homogeneity 58
  The Hungarian Revolution 27

individual and 68, 70
instituted society *see* instituted society
instituting society *see* instituting society
Korean War 22
politics 86
power and discourse 123
psyche and 52–7, 69–70
radical imagination 67
Russian society 17–18
social change 74
social-historical dimension 32, 47
socialism 30
social meaning and institutions 72
SouB 31
subject and 71
theory of discourse 93
Soviet capitalism 17
structuralism 30
subject,
  Castoriadis' work,
    agency 70
    creative psychical capacity and society 70
    historical dimension 65–6
    imagination 118
    leaning on explanation 47
    radical imagination 66–7
    social-historical creation 67
    unconscious 66
  Foucault's work,
    Dews' view 120–1
    Freud's approach 117
    imagination 118
    oneiric world and dreams 117
    The Order of Things 116

panoptic power 120
power, effects of 119
psychoanalysis and ethnology 116
psychological irregularities 120
reciprocity 122
society and social change 122
Williams view 121
subjectification,
  Foucault's view 107, 115, 117
  genealogy 102
  interpretations 122
  panoptic power 120
  power, effects of 119
  social-historical dimension 139
  space of interiority 119–20
  and subjection 120
subjectivity,
  body 101
  Castoriadis power 110
  Castoriadis' understanding of 71
  democracy 78, 86
  Foucault power 108
  genealogy 105
  individualization 106
  instituting power 76
  The Order of Things 98
  power-discourse matrix 93
  power, relationships of 102
  psychoanalysis 136
  space of interiority 119
  transcendentalism 135
  transformation of power 122
  working class 13

teukhein 56–7